Conquer Your Stress
with Mind/Body
Techniques

Kathy Gruver
PhD, LMT, CHt, RM

LOTUS PRESS
Box 325, Twin Lakes, WI 53181 USA
email: lotuspress@lotuspress.com
website: www.LotusPress.com

First Lotus Press Edition 2016
ISBN: 978-0-9406-7638-1

Library of Congress Control Number: 2016941424

Printed in the United States of America

For information address:

LOTUS
PRESS

Lotus Press
Box 325, Twin Lakes, WI 53181 USA
email: lotuspress@ lotuspress.com
website: www.LotusPress.com

Previously Published by:
INFINITY PUBLISHING

Previously Published ISBN: 978-0-7414-9619-5

What people are saying about
Body/Mind Therapies for the Bodyworker:

If only everyone would honestly ask "Who's the Matter with Me?" and recognize that it is usually you, yourself, we would all be better. Meanwhile, as Kathy reveals, body workers may help a great deal more than mind workers!

C. Norman Shealy, M.D., Ph.D.
President, Holos Institutes of Health
Founding President, American Holistic Medical Association
Author of MEDICAL INTUITION, ENERGY MEDICINE, and
BLISS—DOING GOOD TO SELF and OTHERS

Kathy Gruver is a life-long learner dedicated to holistic wellness and the bodywork profession. She's poured her knowledge – and heart and soul- into this text. There are gems of insight here for everyone from practitioners to clients. My hope is readers will honor Gruver by enjoying this text and living well.

Leslie A Young, PhD
Editor-in-Chief,
Massage and Bodywork Magazine

Dr. Kathy Gruver writes in a candid, down-to-earth style that makes it easy to comprehend her powerful message. She provides logical and inspirational information for bodyworkers to elevate their level of wellness and that of their clients. The relevancy of mind/body dynamics that Dr. Gruver brings to light reaches all of us.

David J. Pesek, Ph.D.
Holistic Healthcare Pioneer

I am very lucky to have had Dr. Gruver as a college professor, mentor and friend. After reading her book it was very evident that her experience and education in the wellness field combined with her love of people shines through. Through her extensive knowledge and wonderful humor even those who are unfamiliar with bodywork will be able to take away important lessons that are essential to their life. It is a must read from the doctor to the laymen, you will laugh, learn and remember that good health begins with you.

Jessica Robinett, massage therapist

I am sitting here reading your book and I feel like you are sitting here talking to me. I love it! It is written so well and it is very easy to comprehend. I just read about BioDots, which sound really cool. I know some people who could really benefit from a lot of this book. This is a weekend of taxes and cleaning out OLD papers. I think I will take time for a "mini."

Barbara Begg, retired teacher

Table of Contents

Dedication

This book is dedicated to anyone who struggles with stress and wants to learn about how the mind/body connection can work for them.

Thanks to Hilary Hope at Hope Unlimited for the fabulous cover and Linda Blue Photography for an amazing headshot for the back.

And the lovely people who gave me wisdom for the back cover, Darya Bronston, Dr. Fabrizio Benedetti, Deborah Hutchison, Steven Brynoff.

More thanks to Peter Wright, Fran Lewbel, Dr. Jay Fortman, Jane Hendler, Linda Croyle, TJ Fortuna, Steven Brynoff, Lori Guynes and Sylvia Perlee for contributing their wisdom to this book. And Maria Santos for helping with the index.

A huge thanks to Herbert Benson, Peg Baim, and the Benson-Henry Institute for Mind Body Medicine at Harvard. The time I spent with them and what I learned was invaluable and contributed so much to my life and this book.

And the biggest thanks goes to my husband, Michael Cervin. Without his love and support and constant supply of iced tea (and wine), I could not accomplish half the things I do. I love you wholly with my mind and my body!

Kathy Gruver, PhD
Santa Barbara, CA
Spring 2013

In memory of George K and Dawn H, two amazing clients I lost this year who showed me nothing but support even in their final days.

For your Information

A lot of the techniques I discuss in this book take much training and dedication to learn. Please seek out a qualified practitioner to work with when exploring these new modalities. And if your first experience with a certain method doesn't work for you, try someone else. Many practitioners have different ways of doing the same thing.

And I realize that not everything I talk about will resonate with every reader. I don't advocate any one modality or technique over the other, I'm just giving you a buffet of mind/body options. Take what works for you. And please use a clean plate each time.

Also, a reminder that I am **NOT** a medical doctor and this book is not meant to take the place of your health care provider. I am not intending to diagnose or treat any illness.

A quote from *The Teaching of Buddha.*

II The Theory of Mind-Only

1. Both delusion and Enlightenment originate within the mind, and every existence or phenomenon arises from the functions of the mind, just as different things appear from the sleeves of a magician.

3. Therefore, all things are primarily controlled and ruled by the mind, and are created up by the mind.

One who is able to enjoy the purity of both body and mind walks the path to Buddhahood.

Foreword

Not much has changed since I first wrote *Conquer your Stress* in 2013. Stress is still a pervasive problem in our world. With global and regional unrest, political turmoil and sometimes all-around chaos. It's often difficult to find the stillness in the storm. What has changed is that more and more people are turning to mindfulness and stress reduction practices. The year 2015 was deemed the 'Year of Mindfulness' and many people started to realize the benefits. It's my hope that the medical community embraces mind/body techniques and acknowledges the phenomenal research being done in this field. Some day I hope they prescribe meditation over medication.

In the mean time, I have been meditating more and more. I actually did a 3-day silent retreat, during which time I did daily meditations including a two-hour session. So if you think you can't meditate…take it from me, you absolutely can. I had the true privilege of helping develop a stress reduction program for the military and have had the honor of speaking more on stress and its solutions around the world. So, though we can't necessarily change what's happening out **there**. We can change what is happening in **here**, in our own thoughts, in our own actions. We have the power to respond rather than react. Make a different choice. To quote W.L. Bateman, "If you keep on doing what you have always done, you will always get what you've always got." I hope this book inspires you to make changes!

Thanks to Lotus Press and Santosh and Shanta for the opportunity to share my message of mind/body medicine with even more people.

Have a healthy day!

Kathy Gruver,
Santa Barbara, CA | May 2016

Introduction

Thanks so much for reading *Conquer Your Stress with Mind/Body Therapies.* You are holding this book in your hand, so obviously you care about your health. You know that stress is considered a killer in our society. It's believed that 60-80% of doctor's visits are due to stress-related illness. But here's the interesting thing.

Stress isn't the problem!

I'll say it again. Stress is <u>not</u> the problem. Do you know why? Because we can't control the stress. That is the definition of stress; the perception that demands are exceeding our resources. If we could change and control the stress, it wouldn't be stress. So, if stress isn't the problem, what is you may ask? Good question. It's our reaction to that stress and <u>that</u> we can control. We can't control the layoffs, the fiscal cliff, the traffic and the woman in front of us at the post office that has to look at every stamp ever printed before she finally decides on the flowers. We can't control any of that. But we can control our reaction to it. And that's what I'm going to teach you to do.

   We also have to remember that different people find different things stressful. For example, for fun I like ride rollercoasters, go scuba diving and skydiving. I've also swum with sharks and flown on a trapeze. Many people find these things to be incredibly stress inducing. That good stress that we like is called eustress. And as Hans Selye, stress researcher said, "Stress can only be avoided by dying." And others make the distinction between DIS-stress and stress. We are all predisposed to a certain amount of stress hardiness and we all have different coping mechanisms. Some people thrive on being first responders and have no problem dealing with blood and protruding bones. Others faint at the sign of a needle. To quote Hans Selye again, "As I have often said, I don't think anyone should try to eliminate stress; rather you should find your own stress level, find out to what extent you're really sufficiently resistant to keep a certain level of activity. Also, you have to find a goal you can respect – it doesn't matter if other people respect it. You have to have to have enough independence to be your own judge as to whether your aim is right or wrong." [1]

We all have stress just like we all have a temperature. The issue becomes when it's out of control. Whatever your level of stress hardiness, we all have to find ways to cope with the stress, when it gets out of hand and starts to overtake us. Here you'll learn easy techniques that you can do on your own, for less stress (response). And then I throw in techniques that practitioners can do for/with you for even more relaxation and enhancement of the mind/body connection. You can take control and not allow stress to be in charge of your life. Thank you for embarking on this journey with me. I'll be here for you every step of the way to make sure you get the most out of this book. It's written for you, to help you be healthier and take full advantage of this phenomenal life we have. Welcome.

---

[1] Hans Selye: President, International Institute of Stress, Montreal Canada. Accepted for Publication: Dec. 1979, printed from Journal of Extension: May/June 1988.

Why I Wrote This Book

How I came to be interested in mind/body is an interesting journey all its own. I've been involved in massage for over twenty years and although we think of massage as a purely physical modality, we can't escape recognizing the role of the mind and the spirit in the healing process. The more bodies I put my hands on, the more I saw the connection between what people were saying and thinking, and what was being acted out in their physiology. Carolyn Myss, a five-time *New York Times* bestselling author and internationally renowned speaker in the fields of human consciousness, spirituality and mysticism, health, energy medicine, and the science of medical intuition, describes this phenomenon when she said, "Our biography becomes our biology." And I have definitely seen this to be true.

What I was observing in my practice piqued my interest to go further than just massage and I started investigating. I debated about chiropractic or physical therapy school. But nothing was ringing true to me. I heard the word naturopath and after seeing the definition, knew it was my path. But even after I achieved that goal, I wanted more. After I finished my ND as a traditional naturopath, I pursued a Masters and PhD in Natural Health. Through all those classes and degrees, I began to learn more and more about the mind/body connection. Add to that numerous classes at Harvard Medical School on the topic and my own reading for fun, (Yeah, I read medical books for fun, doesn't everyone?) I began to learn some theories and develop some of my own about health that proved true almost every time I used them in my practice.

First off, there is no separating the mind and the body. We cannot think and believe things without them affecting us in some significant way. If we tell ourselves enough times that we are worthless or stupid or sick or unhappy, we will start to physically exhibit symptoms of such. In the same way, by incorporating positive self-talk, visualizations and affirmations, we can cause positive changes in our bodies and our lives. I will also discuss research and current studies that back up this theory and teach us how to heal the connection between the mind and the body. You can't talk about the body/mind without mentioning the placebo effect and we'll delve into that as well. If studies aren't your thing or you find them intimidating, no worries just skip over those sections in the book. But to me, the studies illustrate how mainstream this thinking has become and I encourage you to at least peruse them.

I also strongly believe that stress is by far the biggest disease we are facing. (I know I just told you a few paragraphs ago that stress isn't the problem, but for the rest of the book I'm going to use the word stress as opposed to stress response, you'll know what I mean.) And I'm not alone in this belief. Early in human history, the stress response, which we'll get into detail on later, was a necessary function for our survival. In modern society it is not quite as useful as it used to be and is often times, in fact, detrimental to our health. Dr. Herbert Benson coined the phrase Relaxation Response in opposition to the stress response. I will teach you ways to utilize the Relaxation Response, not only for your health, but for that of your friends and family as well.

I have also found that not only does negative language and thought affect us, but often our stress gathers in certain vulnerable parts of the body, which seem to have phrases that correspond. For example, if we feel like our hands are full, we might manifest hand pain or carpal tunnel syndrome. This was one of the first client examples that made me aware of this mind/body connection. Author, Louise Hay has similar theories about dis-ease (out of ease) and how its location in different parts of the body corresponds to stresses. I've taken it a step further and will give you ways to uncover these verbal hints for more complete healing. Welcome to the world of the mind/body; let's see if we can learn what the / really means.

As a Resource

I am available to hold workshops and assist in the teaching of this material. So, if your office, corporation, women's festival or retreat can use this type of work, just contact me for more information. I'd love to help.

drkathygruver@gmail.com

Warning Signs of Stress

We all assume we know when we are feeling stress, but here's a comprehensive list of "symptoms" that you might not connect to stress:

<u>Physical symptoms:</u>

Headaches
Indigestion
Stomachaches
Sweaty palms
Sleep difficulty
Dizziness

Back pain
Tight neck and shoulders
Racing heart
Tiredness
Ringing in the ears
Restlessness

<u>Behavioral symptoms</u>

Excess smoking
Bossiness
Compulsive gum chewing
Critical attitude of others

Grinding of teeth
Overuse of alcohol
Compulsive eating
Inability to get things done

<u>Emotional symptoms</u>

Crying
Nervousness/anxiety
Boredom, meaningless
Edginess, ready to explode
Feeling powerless to
  change things

Overwhelming sense of
  pressure
Anger
Loneliness
Unhappiness for no reason
Easily upset

<u>Cognitive symptoms</u>

Trouble thinking clearly
Forgetfulness
Lack of creativity
Memory loss

Inability to make decisions
Thoughts of running away
Constant worry
Loss of sense of humor

Why Now?

America is sicker than ever. Today's youth is the first generation that is believed to not outlive their parents. I just read that women's life expectancy has lessened. Obesity and type 2-diabetes are considered epidemics. Illnesses such as diarrhea, pneumonia, the flu and infection that once claimed the most lives are now, for the most part, under control. Yet diseases of lifestyle are limiting our lifespan. Things that could be changed like diet and exercise habits aren't. We, as a country, are making horrible choices that are impacting our health. What we call healthcare is no more than disease management and though we give plenty of lip service to prevention, we aren't doing much of it.

More and more people are becoming disenchanted with the Western perspective on health. They are tired of seeing pharmaceutical commercials in between every TV show. They are fed up with getting seven minutes to see their doctors, especially when the average time of interruption is 18-23 seconds. They are tired of rising healthcare costs and diminished care. People want to take more control and are turning to complementary alternative medicine for help.

We are seeing a resurgence of people turning to simpler, more traditional ways of healing. Things like herbs, acupuncture and massage are becoming more of a way of life for people and I'm seeing more folks also looking to the medicine of the mind in the way of yoga, meditation and cognitive pursuits. Things that used to be reserved for the "fringe, kooky" healer are now becoming popular, tested and mainstream. Now is the time to take control, to take charge and to reclaim your health. *Conquer Your Stress* will help. You can change your own life. Are you ready?

Introduction to Mind/Body Medicine

True health must encompass all aspects of the person; body, mind and spirit. The power of the mind, language and thoughts are more powerful than people realize. This section of the book excerpted from my doctoral dissertation explains the history of mind/body techniques, contemporary perspectives about its use and cites some of the amazing scientific studies that have been done on this topic. If some of this scientific research can be brought to the mainstream and presented in a cohesive and coherent fashion, healthcare can be drastically altered for the better. We have certainly heard of the placebo effect and have been exposed to phrases like "think positive" and "the power of the mind" (mainly on bumper stickers), but the average citizen has not been truly educated about the power of his and her thoughts. These techniques can shed light on the power inherent in everyone and illustrate the untapped ability of the body to heal itself. Easily learned methods like creative visualization, self-hypnosis and positive self-talk give power to the individual and can possibly change people's bodies and health. Is it just the placebo? In this next section you'll learn that it might not even matter.

A History of Mind/Body Medicine

In the past, placebos (from the Latin "I shall please") may have been given to please or placate patients, to distinguish "real" ailments from those that were "imagined" or "psychosomatic" or even worse, to distinguish "genuine" patients from "malingerers."[2] It was thought if a patient responded to the placebo, then they were clearly making up their illness. After all, the placebo doesn't do anything. Or so they thought.

The placebo effect had never been given so much attention until Beecher's *The Powerful Placebo* was published in 1955, stating that the placebo was effective in 35% of patients.[3] Since then medical professionals and laypeople alike have been debating the importance of this phenomenon. Though Beecher's study has been criticized the past 15 years as statistically incorrect and containing much research bias,[4] there is no argument that his groundbreaking paper has at least made scientists question this phenomenon. Meanwhile, researchers have moved so far forward as to image the brain to see what sections are activated by the placebo and have proven that it is not only all in one's head, but in the brain as well. Studies have also shown that placebo treatments are effective for specific ailments like pain, depression, skin conditions and asthma. There is no doubt as humankind moves into the future of the placebo that more evidence will surface regarding its multitude of benefits.

[2] Crow, J. (2006). The placebo response. *Practice Nurse, 31*(12), 27-30.

[3] Beecher, H. (1955). The Powerful Placebo. *Journal of American Medical Association.* 159(17):1602-6.

[4] Kienle, G., Kiene, H. (1997). The powerful placebo: Fact or fiction? Journal of Clinical Epidemiology, 50(12), 1311-1318. (As cited by Nimmo, 2005).

As the concept of the placebo grew in the minds of scientists, the mind/body connection was gaining ground in the mainstream. One of the pioneers of the self-help movement, Louise Hay published a book in 1988 that explained the mental causes of physical disease.[5] Since its publication, a multitude of laypeople and doctors alike have explored the mind's effect on the physical structure. The book *Healing Words* [6] by Texas physician, Larry Dossey, explains what the power of prayer can do for healing and cites cases of cancer going into remission and miracles of healing occurring. Dossey encourages a strong relationship with the physician, prayer, visualization and hypnosis. Dr. John Sarno, a professor of rehabilitation medicine, coined the phrase "tension myositis syndrome" (TMS) as what happens to the muscles in the body from suppressed anger and emotions.[7] He believes that by working through the feelings, the pain will diminish. These pioneers of healing brought to the mainstream that the mind could have power over the body.

German physician, Franz Anton Mesmer introduced hypnosis, one of the oldest mind/body techniques, in the 18th century.[8] His technique of hypnosis, then called animal magnetism, has grown from swinging a shiny object in front of a "victim" during a stage performance to a viable healing technique. As early as 1843, hypnosis was used in France as a popular method for reducing pain.[9] Whether self-hypnosis, suggestions from a therapist or recorded on MP3, hypnosis

---

[5] Hay, L. (1988). *Heal Your Body*. Santa Monica: Hay House Inc.

[6] Dossey, L. (1993). *Healing Words*. New York: HarperCollins Publishers.

[7] Sarno, J. (1991). *Healing Back Pain. The Mind-Body Connection*. New York: Warner Books.

[8] Dossey, L. (2000). Hypnosis: A window into the soul of healing. *Alternative Therapies, 6*(2), 12-17, 102-104.

[9] Sharma, S., Kaur, J. (2006). Hypnosis and pain management. *Nursing Journal of India, 97*(6), 129-131.

has gained ground in the scientific arena as a valid medical treatment.

A 1996 panel survey of attendees at a NIH (National Institutes of Health) conference found strong evidence that hypnosis helped alleviate pain associated with cancer.[10] Hypnosis, having been in and out of favor for centuries, holds true today as one option for furthering the power of the mind over the body. Many other non-pharmacological options are available for pain relief. Just a few are progressive muscle relaxation, guided imagery and aromatherapy (see future chapter).[11]

Guided imagery (or creative visualization) is similar to hypnosis. There have been daydreamers as long as there have been humans on earth. But creative visualization is tapping into those fantasies and creating them materially in the real world. Whether this is for healing, tumor shrinking or finding a parking space, the mind is credited with incredible power to create change in the material world. Almost every culture has imagery-based rituals which could be considered the oldest medicine there is.[12] The ancient Greeks actually considered the imagination to be an organ. If the brain believes it, there is nothing to stop the body from following through with the imagined instructions that are given to it. This is called top-down as opposed the bottom-up. If you burn your finger and then your brain interprets the signals of pain, this is a bottom-up event. However, if you are driving and you think about a horrible car accident and start feeling stress, this is a top-down event. The brain tends

---

[10] National Institutes of Health. (1996). Integration of behavioral and relaxation approaches into the treatment of chronic pain and insomnia. NIH Technology Assessment Panel on Integration of Behavioral and Relaxation Approaches into the Treatment of Chronic Pain and Insomnia. *JAMA, 276*(4), 313-318.

[11] Valente, S. (2006). Hypnosis for pain management. *Journal of Psychosocial Nursing, 44*(2), 23-30.

[12] Horrigan, B. (2002). Marty Rossman, MD. Imagery: The body's natural language for healing. *Alternative Therapies, 8*(1), 81-89.

to interpret these top-down events as if this situation is really happening. The mind will order the same fight or flight response and the body will react.

If there is any doubt about the connection between body and thoughts and the validity of top-down processes, the following three examples should be pretty convincing. One is the concept of hysterical pregnancy or pseudocyesis. This is when a woman (or man) starts to have biological changes that indicate pregnancy; with one exception...there is no baby. This disorder has been known to exist since documented medicine and the historic Queen Mary Tudor was believed to have experienced two episodes.[13] Estimates of prevalence range from 1 in 250 to 1-6 in 22,000.[14] Though it happens at all ages, not surprisingly it is most common in women of childbearing age. "This is one of the classical examples in medicine of how the mind affects the rest of the body."[15]

Turning away from medicine and to the church, the history of exorcism is another example of mind over matter. Exorcisms were being used up to 200 years before the placebo effect in medicine and "trick trials" were used frequently to test for true possession.[16] With the right combination of Latin and holy water, the demon would miraculously leave the victim. Clearly the church understood the connection between the mind and the body. It is to be

---

[13] Whelan, C., Stewart, D. (1990). Pseudocyesis: A review and report of six cases. *International Journal of Psychiatry in Medicine*, 20, 97-108. (As cited in Rosch, 2002).

[14] Waldman, A., Marquese, M., Greer, R. (1992). Pseudocyesis in a schizophrenic woman of childbearing age. *Psychosomatics*, 33, 360-361. (As cited in Rosch, 2002).

[15] Harland, R., Warner, N. (1997). Delusions of pregnancy in the elderly. *International Journal of Geriatric Psychiatry*, 123, 115-117. (As cited in Rosch, 2002).

[16] Kaptchuk, T., Kerr, C., Zanger, A. (2009). The Art of Medicine: Placebo controls, exorcisms and the devil. *Lancet*, 374(9697), 1234-1235.

noted that even today the Catholic Church performs exorcisms and takes this procedure very seriously.

Another related area where belief plays more of a role than reality is the area of voodoo death. Villagers who were believed to be cursed by the "medicine man" would start to react physically and once the "bone was shaken at them," there was no chance for life.[17] A researcher shares, "So rooted is this belief on the part of the patient, that some enemy has 'pointed' the bone at him, that he will actually lie down to die, and succeed in the attempt, even at the expense of refusing food and succour (assistance) within his reach: I have myself witnessed three or four such cases."[18] "The question which now arises is whether an ominous and persistent state of fear can end the life of man."[19] An intriguing issue, it questions the far-reaching effect of the body/mind connection and what the future of the concept holds for human healing. It is clear that throughout time there has been some awareness of the connection of mind and body, even if little was understood. The future of this issue could very well be total healing of the public at large. If it can be documented that the words one chooses for themselves and others can change brain function and physiology, then the power to heal lies within the individual. The future of medicine could be a prescription for words and images rather than pills and surgery.

[17] Cannon, W. (1957). "Voodoo" Death. *Psychosomatic Medicine, XIX*(3), 182-190.

[18] Roth, W. (1897). *Ethnological Studies among the North-West-Central Queensland Aborigines,* (Brisbane and London), p. 154. (As cited by Cannon, 1957).

[19] Cannon, W. (1957). "Voodoo" Death. *Psychosomatic Medicine, XIX*(3), 182-190.

What are the Implications of Mind/Body Medicine?

"Just because we don't understand it, doesn't mean it isn't happening," comments Susan Casey of *O Magazine* while a guest on *CNN's Anderson Cooper 360°*. She and Dr. Sanjay Gupta were discussing the case of a faith healer named John of God. "Is he giving false hope? I don't think there is such a thing," says Casey. "He seems to get results." Jeff Rediger, a Harvard Instructor in Psychiatry visited the healer and couldn't figure out how he does it. "I expected to see slight of hand and there was some of that, but people got better." Follow up tests with modern Western equipment confirmed that these people were actually healed.[20]

Is it purely belief in the healing that causes changes in our physiology? How much affect do words, thoughts and expectations have on our healing? These questions have been asked for centuries and several new schools of thought answer, "Yes" and "A lot." Scientologists take in this theory in something called Dianetic auditing. They believe that everything that happens to a person is imprinted and can cause physical and emotional repercussions. From the time of birth, traumas called "engrams" are recorded and influence everyone the rest of their lives. Until of course, they "run them out" using a technique called auditing. Hubbard coined the word Dianetics that means, "What the mind is doing to the body." Or more precisely "relating to thought."[21] Through verbally reenacting these negative experiences over and over again, they can be cleared from the body and spirit, leaving room for the positive and healthy. In 2001, the American Religious Identification Survey (ARIS) reported that there were 55,000 adults in the

---

[20] Viewed 12-22-10, TV show, *Anderson Cooper 360°*

[21] http://oxforddictionaries.com/definition/english/Dianetics

United States who consider themselves Scientologists.[22] Regardless of Tom Cruise's couch jumping, so many followers of Scientology claim complete healing from physical and mental disease. Faith in the connection of the mind and body is not as fringe as it used to be. Currently there are 41,900,000 entries on Google when searching the words "mind/body medicine," 23,300,000 for "affirmations," 5,670,000 for "positive thought" and 2,630,000 for "placebo effect."[23] It is not simply the advent of the computer that is expanding this knowledge.

The popular radio station NPR (National Public Radio) addresses subjects like this all the time. A recent interview, *Neurotheology: This is Your Brain on Religion,*[24] discussed how different parts of the brain light up during meditation and studies have been showing it is a cumulative process with the benefits growing over time. Another program on the station called *All Things Considered* looked at the effect of prayer on another person.[25] No one can explain how praying for another person could actually effect change in their physiology but new studies at the University of Wisconsin may be able to prove they do. In this study, husbands, wired to monitoring equipment, looked at photos of their wives and projected loving healing thoughts on them. In another room, the wife sat wired to sensitive devices that measure blood flow, temperature, and blood pressure. When the husband gazed at his wife, the measurement line of his monitor became ragged and his nervous system reacted. Within two seconds, the wife had the same physiological reaction. They repeated this procedure with thirty-six couples each time rendering the

---

[22] http://www.infoplease.com/ipa/A0922574.html

[23] Searched 7/20/16 on www.google.com

[24] Conan, N. (2010, December 15). [Interview with Dr. Andrew Newberg] *NPR's Talk of the Nation* radio interview.

[25] Hagerty, B. (2009, May 21). [Interview with Dr. Schlitz and Dr. Radin]. *NPR's All Things Considered* radio show.

same results. The odds of that happening were 1 in 11,000.[26] Quantum physics theory of entanglement may offer an explanation; that everything in the universe is infinitely connected.

Quantum physics itself has become a mainstream topic with the production of the movie *What the Bleep do We Know: Down the Rabbit Hole.*[27] This film discusses connections of the mind and body through occurrences such as telepathy, distance healing, and precognition, and interviews cutting edge scientists and philosophers about this vast connection between aspects of human beings. They explain that the hypothalamus makes peptides, which turn into amino acids and form proteins, which are vastly affected by chemicals triggered by our emotions. One can become addicted to these chemicals, thus addicted to these emotions. This could explain why someone is always in pain, in the same relationship with the same type of gal, in the same bad job, and cannot heal his or her physical body. It also illustrates how the emotions have a physical reaction in our bodies.

But to become aware of our thoughts takes an enormous amount of awareness and concentration. Humans lose awareness every six to ten seconds. This may be why so many can't meditate and claim to be unable to heal and affect change in their lives. The brain processes 400 billion bits of information per second with awareness of only 2000 per second.[28] By increasing that awareness, the possibilities are endless of what the mind can do. A recent book called

---

[26] Hagerty, B. (2009, May 21). [Interview with Dr. Schlitz and Dr. Radin]. NPR's All Things Considered radio show.

[27] Vicente, M., Chasse, B, Arnitz, W. (Producers). (2004). *What the Bleep? Down the Rabbit Hole.* [Motion Picture]. United States: 20th Century Fox.

[28] Vicente, M., Chasse, B, Arnitz, W. (Producers). (2004). *What the Bleep? Down the Rabbit Hole.* [Motion Picture]. United States: 20th Century Fox.

Free Will[29] by Sam Harris theorizes that we don't even have free will at all. We can make a decision, but when did we decide to decide? Why wine over beer? Well, I like wine better, but why? Where is the freedom in that? He poses some interesting questions and I suggest reading his book for a fascinating take on free will and mind/body connection.

Through meditation it is believed that one can change their bodies. Through prayer one can help others heal. Many philosophers are now tapping into this theory for business. Books like *Think and Grow Rich*[30] tell us we can be successful in business using our minds. *The Answer*[31] explains how to use affirmations, vision boards and self-talk to achieve wealth and dreams in business. The popular movie *The Secret* (2006) shares three tips to manifesting anything:

1. Ask. Tell the universe what you want.
2. Believe. You do not need to know how it will happen, just know it will.
3. Receive. This works for health, wealth, love, even parking spaces.

Many physicians are recommending affirmations for healing cancer and HIV; they speak of strengthening the relationship between doctor and patient and going back to the days of healing and not just impersonally prescribing drugs. Drs. Dossey[32] and Siegel[33] have written extensively about their experiences with spontaneous healing, more comfortable deaths and patients beating the odds because of

---

[29] Harris, S. (2012) *Free Will*. New York: Free Press.

[30] Hill, N. (1937). *Think and Grow Rich*. New York: Tribeca Books.

[31] Assarar, J., Smith, M. (2008). *The Answer*. New York: First Atria Books.

[32] Dossey, L. (1993). *Healing Words*. New York: HarperCollins Publishers.

[33] Siegel, B. (1989). *Peace, Love and Healing*. New York: Harper and Row, Inc.

18

the power of their minds and will. They both list meditations for healing, how to talk with your doctor and how affirmations and prayer can change the body for the better. Dr. Andrew Weil writes in great detail about curing warts with hypnosis, biofeedback and how those who are adept at yoga have incredible control over their physical beings. "Possibly, some physical limitations we now accept as immutable constraints on the human body are, in fact, plastic and subject to the power of the mind."[34] By plastic he means changeable.

This is not just the realm of open-minded physicians. Throughout time various religions have touted the power of the mind, mainly the Eastern schools of thought like Buddhism and Taoism. Some people arrive at these lifestyles, not through religion, but through experience. Louise Hay, author of *Heal Your Body,* formed her theories on mind/body connection through observing life. Her little blue book, as it was called, points out the connection between certain physical dis-ease (out of ease) states and what thought process or mind set might have led to it.

For example, joints represent changing directions and accepting new experiences. She then lists an affirmation, "I easily flow with new experiences, new directions and new changes."[35] Eye problems correspond with not liking what you see in your own life with the affirmation of "I see with love and joy." Bowel problems represent fear of letting go of the old and things no longer needed. She recommends the affirmation, "I freely and easily release the old and joyously welcome the new." Her 84-page book lists every ailment you can think of and it ends with her saying "I love you."

In a controversial study, doctor of alternative medicine, Masaru Emoto, tested the concept that words can

---

[34] Weil, A. (2004). *Health and Healing*. Boston: Houghton Mifflin Company.
[35] Hay, L. (1988). *Heal Your Body*. Santa Monica: Hay House Inc.

affect human physiology.[36]. Words were spoken to or taped to a bottle of water. Afterwards, the water was frozen and the crystalline structure of the water was examined under a microscope. It was then judged on the beauty and formation of the crystals.

It is clear from his study that negative words and sounds affect the water differently than the positive words. His study shows a remarkable level of beauty and symmetry in the water crystals that received positive words and messages in contrast to chaotic and unattractive crystal patterns in the water that received negative messaging. If his study is accurate and one really can change water structure with just thoughts and words, and humans are 60-70 % water, the implications for the physical body are astronomical. Examples of his results can be found on line on various blogs or his book, *The Hidden Messages in Water.*

Consider this concept in regards to daily life and the potential influence of those around you. Someone's negative words (or music) might be creating negative health in their friends and neighbors. I think this partially may explain how we can walk into a room and feel that someone is in a bad mood or just fought with their spouse without even seeing their face. It's as if the energy hangs in the air. Who knows how his concept of water and emotion might lend credibility to our "sixth sense."

The best studied of the mind/body connection is the placebo. The current challenge with the placebo effect is proving its existence in an ethical and effective way. It is difficult to do a double blind placebo controlled study if what is being studied IS the placebo. Dr. Benedetti at the University of Turin, one of the leading researchers in the neurobiology of placebos, and other researchers offer some

[36] Emoto, M. (2001) *The Hidden Messages in Water.* Hillsboro, OR: Atria Books.

solutions by suggesting open vs. hidden treatments.[37] In this type of study you may be given a painkiller, but from a machine behind a curtain so you don't know it is being administered. Contrarily, you might be told you are receiving morphine when you are actually being treated with saline in your IV. Which treatment do you react better to? The results may surprise you.

Another method of testing the placebo is the triple blind study where one group gets an active drug, one the placebo and one no treatment at all. More research has certainly been done recently on how to use our minds and the placebo effect to heal. Some studies involving sham surgery or hidden vs. open treatment are starting to gain attention and make scientists and doctors pause and consider the possibilities.[38] As more researchers acknowledge the power of positive thinking and the placebo effect, better-designed studies will appear in the literature. More phenomenal information about placebos can be found in Benedetti's book, *Placebo Effects, Understanding the Mechanisms in Health and Disease.*[39]

Not everyone believes in this type of healing. Websites and books try to "debunk" the charlatans. However, with so much information proving it exists, how much longer will people be able to debate things like the placebo effect for healing? Perhaps it is simply the threat that this kind of information holds to Western medicine and the drug companies at large. Or maybe humanity is simply not ready for this type of information since it requires personal responsibility and hard work to change. Perhaps when someone tells you it's all in your head; maybe that's just where it should be for total healing.

---

[37] Benedetti, F, Colloca, L. (2005). Placebos and painkillers: is mind as real as matter? *Nature Reviews. Neuroscience, 6*(7), 545-552.

[38] Benedetti, F. (2006). Placebo Analgesia. *Neurological Science*, 27, S100-S102.

[39] Benedetti, F. *Placebo Effects, Understanding the Mechanisms in Health and Disease.* Oxford University Press, New York. 2009.

Bringing Mind/Body Medicine to Your Life

Sometimes the words we use can unlock a mystery to what's happening in the body. This is what I discovered in my massage practice about the connection between the body and the mind.

I first discovered the power of the mind/body connection with a client who was having hand and wrist issues. I would do massage and her symptoms would disappear but within days they would return. I was frustrated that she seemed to be at an impasse with her healing. I knew she was doing her "homework"; stretching, ice, vitamins, taking breaks at work, adjusting her workstation, but nothing was helping to affect permanent change in her condition. I was getting irritated that I couldn't get her over that hump and I expressed my frustration to her. We started to discuss her pain and I asked again when it hurt the most. She said, "When I'm gripping things, grasping them. I have trouble holding my hairdryer and I can't lift my wine glass." I thought that was a tragedy so I figured we had to do something, and quickly. Her description ran through my head a few times and I concentrated on the words…. grip, grasp and I asked her, "Is there something you're holding too tightly, is there something you need to let go?" Then I opened my hand.

She looked at me and her answer stunned me. Honestly, the fact that she had an answer at all stunned me. She very soulfully said, "I don't want to let my kids go." She went on to tell me how her brother was killed in a car crash right after he got his driver's license and how that broke apart the family and what it did to her parents. Her kids were now at that age, and she was terrified to give them the freedom she knew they needed. We discussed this a bit further during the rest of the massage, she made another appointment and left. In the time between appointments, she talked about her experience with her husband…and her kids.

She told them the story that she had never shared before and was honest with them about her fear. When I saw her next, her pain had decreased and soon, her treatments lasted longer until she no longer needed to see me. That fear, that need to let go was the final step in her healing.

After my experience with that client, I started to pay more attention to the words and the phrases that clients chose to describe what was happening in their bodies. I also listened, in general, to how they spoke of their lives. Did they constantly speak negatively about their condition and their life? I had one client walk into my office, her very first appointment with me, and say, "My neck's been hurting forever, nothing helps, you probably can't do anything for me….should I take my clothes off?" I thought, "Well, you can give it a shot, but with that attitude, I'm not sure I can help you." During the sessions I tried to encourage her to change her verbiage. If she didn't believe she'd ever feel better, then how could she? I spent just as much time speaking with her about her language as I did her physical condition.

At that time, I was in a class for my master's degree where Louise Hay's book *Heal Your Life* was being used as a text. She was talking about self-love and how every day we should look in the mirror and say, "I love and accept myself just the way I am." This is a very effective tool for self-healing. I mentioned this to my negative client, thinking it could be really beneficial for her. She laughed and said, "Oh, I could never do that…I don't get that whole self-love thing. I mean, what does that even mean?" I was flabbergasted. She could NEVER do that? It struck me as sort of sad, that someone couldn't look in the mirror and say that they loved themselves. How can we not love ourselves?

I pointed out that she swam almost everyday, she ate good food, she played bridge with her friends, she took the time to come see me. I asked if she enjoyed all those things. She answered affirmatively. Then I said, "That is self-love." She got it. I worked with her at great length to reflect on how she talked about her body. If someone asked how she was doing she either answered in the socially correct fashion of "fine" or went on some long tirade about how horrible everything was. I believed that the more she belittled her body and told herself and everyone else how bad it was, it would only be too happy to oblige.

Over time she stopped referring to her neck as stupid, dumb and annoying and began to love every part of herself. She started doing affirmations while she swam, imaging her neck getting stronger with every arm stroke and though I honestly can't say that it reduced her pain; it certainly gave her the ability to deal with it better. Sometimes just changing how we feel about something is healing enough. Positive thoughts can do wonders.

What was interesting about this particular client was how she got to this negative state. She gave birth to a child who was severely brain damaged and he lived for 18 years before he died. He was born in March and died in May. And every year from March to May she would get depressed. She would relive every painful memory, overwhelmed by feelings of guilt, anger, rage, and helplessness. She would welcome those feelings in. She practically scheduled it on the calendar. And though I will talk about how important it is to acknowledge and honor our emotions, reliving something that happened thirty years ago over and over again is not a healthy choice. When I first asked her what she was doing when her neck hurt her, she answered, "I can't turn my head to look back, it hurts." At that point I realized all she was doing was looking back.

To me, the mind is a vast computer and what we seek, we find. It's like typing key words into your search engine of choice. If you're looking for information about massage, you type in massage; if you're looking for cats you type in cats; if you want to read about Brittany Spears you don't type in the words Karl Malden. So, if we are programming our mind for sickness, illness, lack, poverty, suffering, fear and hatred that is exactly what we are going to get. This is where affirmations can be useful. I will discuss affirmations in depth in a separate chapter.

The most important thing is to recognize situations where you tend toward negativity and decide to change your mind. No one can do this for you and often we're not ready to give up the thought process and change. It can be very scary and it's a lot of hard work. But, going in to situations with a negative attitude doesn't benefit anyone and just makes life unpleasant.

Now, how does this help you? Going back to my first example of the woman with the wrist issues. I believe that we could have done all the massage therapy in the world and if she hadn't realized the weight that the emotions were carrying she never would have fully healed. I think that in many cases the ailments and dis-eases from which we suffer in the body are a warning sign that something is out of balance emotionally or spiritually. If we listen to the cues early enough, they won't grow in to big problems like cancer and heart disease. Now, please do not misunderstand, I'm not saying that we can cure everything with just our thoughts or that we are causing our own illnesses. Disease, especially cancer, is very complicated and caused by everything from environmental issues and toxins, to genetics and sometimes what seems to be just plain bad luck. However, if we can work on the emotional issues and be healthy in that realm and it affects even 10% of our healing, why wouldn't we make that choice? If we can enhance the effectiveness of our treatments, I think we would welcome that option.

There have been multitudes of studies done about the placebo effect, our beliefs, the power of prayer and positive thought on healing. We'll discuss a lot of these throughout the book. It can take some effort, certainly, to change a lifetime of beliefs, but the benefits far outweigh the work it will take. If you notice yourself or a loved one consistently being negative, try to gently bring it to their attention. Often we don't even realize the script that we typically use. Words like regret, always, never, bad, stupid, or apologizing for everything are good indications that we are trapped in negative patterns. Still badmouthing a spouse from twenty years ago or blaming their parents at age 52 for their rotten childhood is an indication of being stuck in past, negative patterns. Really observe yourself and try to make changes or say to your friend something like, "I notice when I ask you about your arm you are always negative about it. How might it feel if you changed the way you talk about it? Do you think it's possible that the cycle of pain is continuing partially due to your language about it?" Be careful not to overstep the bounds of friends, tell them what to do, make them feel wrong or stupid or try to play psychologist. (Unless you are actually a psychologist) Those are surefire ways to lose a friend or upset a loved one. Or suggest they go see a mind/body practitioner.

I've also observed, like the woman with the wrist issue, that the area of pain can indicate what is stuck emotionally. Here are a few examples:

-Hand and wrist: get a grip, grasping too tightly, feel like their hands are full
-Low back: support issues, feeling spineless, stabbed in the back, sexual issues
-Lower leg: moving forward, taking the next step
-Neck: Who's the pain in the neck?
-Sciatica: Who's the pain in the butt?

Here's a list I've put together of some of the phrases in this society that have body/mind connections. Do any of these sound familiar to you?

A big mouth
A chip on your shoulder
Big hearted
Bone of contention
Broken hearted
Can't get you out of my head
Can't put my finger on it
Can't stomach it
Cold blooded
Cold feet

Cold shoulder
Cost an arm and a leg
Cross your mind
Doesn't have a leg to stand on
Elbow grease
Elbow your way in
Elbowroom
From the bottom of your heart
Get a leg up
Getting on my nerves
Get off my back
Get under my skin
Give my right arm for…
Going out of my mind/head
Grab the opportunity
Grasping at straws
Greet someone with open arms
Gut feeling (we've all felt this one haven't we?)
Have no backbone
Have your back against the wall
Have heart
He has gall
He's soured to the experience (GERD?)
Heart of gold
Heart set on something
Heart to heart talk
Heartache
Heartbreak
Heartfelt
I can't get a grip
I can't stomach this
I don't have the heart to do it
It's burning me up
It's eating at me (ulcer brewing?)
Jump in with both feet
Keep someone at arm's length
Know it like the back of your hand
Lend a hand

Longs for the sweetness (related to diabetes)
Lose heart
Lump in your throat
Makes me sick to my stomach
Makes my skin crawl
Mouthing off
Moving forward (lower legs)
My hands are full
My heart is blocked (clogged arteries/arteriolosclerosis)
My heart is heavy
My stomach is in knots
No support (back issues)
Now I can breathe easy (feeling of relief, was there asthma
        or bronchitis before?)
Open heart
Open mind
Pain in the ass (piriformis and sciatic issues)
Pain in the neck
Point the finger at someone
Put my foot in my mouth
Put one foot in front of the other
Put your best foot forward
Rug is pulled out from under you
Save face
Shake a leg
Shoot from the hip
Slipped out of my grasp
Someone to lean on
Spineless
Stabbed in the back (pain between the shoulder blades)
Stand on my own two feet
Start off on the wrong foot
Take something to heart
Takes your breath away
To be on your last leg
Tongue-tied
Turn a blind eye
Turn your back on someone

Up to his elbows
Wait on someone hand and foot
Walk the talk
Wears his heart on his sleeve
Weighing on me
Weight of the world is on my shoulders
Welcome someone with open arms
What are you gripping too tightly?
You're such a headache
You've got guts

I also encourage people to avoid saying that something is "killing" them. I don't think that's the best thing to be programming.

Noticing where you are suffering and thinking of these common phrases can help you get to the emotional root of what is causing the pain. Again, I'm not saying pain and illness is 100% emotional. Your back might hurt because you lifted incorrectly or your neck is sore because you cradle the phone against your shoulder. Even with that it can't hurt to investigate the emotional components. There is something called somatization, when there is no clear physical reason for the pain, but there seems to be an emotional link. Somatizers are people whose medical problems are a physical manifestation of emotional conflicts that stay unconscious. Like energy in physics, the stress caused by these conflicts cannot be destroyed, but is transformed into physical symptoms. The physical is a lot more easily dealt with than the emotional. Many people's physical symptoms get worse with stress, but somatizer's pain is almost exclusively connected to the emotions. Tens of billions of dollars a year are spent on medical care for somatizers as they go from doctor to doctor to find out what's wrong.

Here is a personal example, not of somatizing, but of the connection between the thoughts and the physical. I'll be using a lot of personal examples throughout the book.

Several years ago on a Monday morning, I went out to change the water in the birdbath. Something I do every day. That particular day, I lifted the concrete bath and felt searing pain in my low back and heard a squishing noise. It dropped me to my knees <u>and</u> scared the daylights out of me. I was in so much pain I couldn't stand up, let alone replace the birdbath. I crawled into the house crying and called for my husband to get me some ice. I lay on the floor terrified. I remembered all the clients I had that had sustained back injuries and how they couldn't sit, stand, walk, work, drive, have sex, dance, move or function at all and I became very scared. My husband retrieved the ice and called the chiropractor and then asked me what happened. I didn't know. He told me to lie there and figure it out. (I love when he reminds me to do that.) So I did. I lay there thinking about the situation.

What was different about that day? Nothing. What was I doing another way? Nothing. What was I thinking about? <u>That</u> got my attention. At the moment I had done the lifting, I was thinking about my workweek. I had had a few clients that cancelled, which left some gaps in my schedule. For some reason, this time it made me fearful. Fearful that I didn't have enough, that I wouldn't make it, that I had failed. It was a visceral feeling in my gut even as I lay on ice and recounted it. I had to analyze those thoughts. Was it really failure? Did I truly not have enough? Were three clients cancelling actually going to cause my business to fail? Clearly, the answer to that was NO. But for some reason, at that moment, I was vulnerable to that fear.

As I had this realization, warmth spread through my back. I learned many years ago that low back problems are related to money issues, sex issues, and personal relationship and support issues. Wow! The money one hit me, big time. I did some self-talk about the situation, checked my bank account to confirm I wasn't going to be homeless in the next 5 days and told my body it had until Thursday to be better. (Programming recovery time actually does work.) I had massage, chiropractic, ice, ibuprofen and said positive affirmations about my life, my practice and my finances and by Thursday I was fit as a fiddle. This back issue has recurred only two other times, both on Monday mornings and both when I was overly and irrationally concerned about money. Are there times we really have to be concerned about money? Heck yeah! But this time it was fear and insecurity about the subject. It was unfounded, irrational fear. I looked at my bank account and could see that I would be okay with a few less clients that week. This simple observation gave me back control not to mention a well-deserved rest. I wasn't a slave to my feelings anymore.

(Just a note. I've learned that if your body needs rest and you aren't giving it rest, it will make you rest, a cold, an injury, and things getting cancelled. I don't recommend waiting for these things to give you a break, make the choice yourself.)

Now, what is the point of that story? I pinpointed the emotional cause of my issue and erased it, which I believe helped my healing. It illustrated in a very personal way that our emotions and thoughts can affect our body. And most importantly, that no matter how much work I do on this subject, I am vulnerable too!

If you notice that these things apply to you or a practitioner points it out, you might start thinking about other aspects of your life from this perspective. Self-examination, in an honest way, is the cornerstone of health. Sometimes we can't see these things in ourselves and we need a professional to help guide us.

Here's another example. A client came to me with neck pain. (Who is the pain in the neck?) During the course of the massage he was telling me about his newly diagnosed ulcer and that there was burning and then stuff would bubble up. This sounded to me like unexpressed anger so I asked, "Is there something that's eating at you?" This is how the conversation continued.

Me: Ulcer, that sounds awful, is there something that's eating at you?

Him: Well, the doctor said I have too much stomach acid.

Me: Yes, but is there something that is eating away at you?

Him: It seems to be spicy foods.

Me: Sure, but I mean, is there something that is eating at you and then bubbles up to the surface? (I said it more dramatically and with hand gestures this time)

Him: (thinks for a second) Oh, I get it…I see what you're saying. Sure…tomatoes, peppers, garlic….

He wasn't ready to make the leap to connecting the mind and body. I suspected it was the relationship with his boss and interestingly, as soon as he left his job the ulcer started to clear.

Now, I'm not saying we should be running out to leave our job, our wife, etc. Sometimes we can't escape a stressful situation, but we can find ways to deal with it from a positive place. Focus on the positive, whether it's the view from the office, a coworker whom you like or just a paycheck. Focusing on the positive and not dwelling on the negative can sometimes make all the difference in the world. We have three choices in a stressful situation. Leave, change the situation or change your self.

I had a male client who was having horrible low back pain. His job involved lots of climbing around on the floor in uncomfortable positions and heavy lifting. This pain was impacting his ability to do his job. About half way through the massage, after acknowledging that this certainly could be a profession-related issue and that there was a leg length difference and that his piriformis (attaches to the sacrum and top of the femur) and quadratus lumborum (muscles in the low back) certainly were tight, I asked if he found a connection between the level of pain and his stress level. He said there was.

I then mentioned to him that the low back often represented money and personal support issues. He was quiet for a very long time and I wondered if he was pondering, ignoring me or had simply fallen asleep. About twenty minutes went by before he gave me the following response: "Yeah, interesting. I've been pretty stressed about money. My business is pretty slow right now. I'm still working, but I'm afraid of what might happen if I don't get some new clients in." I think it was the first time he vocalized that fear out loud. He then mentioned that he was also afraid to tell his wife. He let out a big sigh and I felt his body relax a few degrees. He didn't want to be seen as a failure or make her worry. I suggested that perhaps sharing that with her might decrease the stress he was feeling. Perhaps they could meet the issue head on and she could support him emotionally through the fear that he was feeling. He agreed.

The next time I saw him, there had been some improvement in his pain level. His muscles were less tight and in general, he seemed happier. He had shared his concerns with his wife over dinner that previous week and they had a great conversation about finances and his job. After putting pen to paper and working some things out, they realized that even if he never got busier, they would still be perfectly fine, and it brought them closer.

I could have just massaged him and helped his back from the physical aspect, but by asking a few questions, he was able to find deeper healing. It can be that simple. We might just have to ask the body what the pain is trying to tell us and then listen for the answer.

People have asked me why everyone doesn't have low back pain then, since the issues connected to it are universal. And that is a very valid question. What I've observed is that the pain often manifests when it is a long-term, unacknowledged emotional issue, a habitual thought or something very threatening and acute like my sudden money fear. Once we process the emotion and start to feel in control, the pain and the emotional pattern ends. You will most likely still need to do the physical things like massage, chiropractic, ice, etc. Clearing the emotional pattern can also bring healing and we'll explore numerous techniques to do just that.

Remember that for true health, we need to balance all aspects of body, mind and spirit. And perhaps some of our physical manifestations of illness have an emotional trigger. Affirmations can help, as can analyzing what situations we treat from a negative mindset. Our words and thoughts have a larger influence on our physicality than we realize. If we can integrate the emotions with the physical, perhaps we can achieve full and long lasting healing.

Once we pay attention to the connection of the mind/body in one area, it leaks to other areas of our lives as well. I bet when my client experiences future illnesses, he might examine those from a mind/body perspective as well. Doing so, can help heal all aspects of life.

Speaking of healing, let's talk about healing vs. curing. Now, according to my license and the FDA/AMA, I'm not allowed to be curing. That word alone can get me in big trouble, but I'm going to use it here for my purposes. (Don't tell.) The word *cure* comes from the root meaning, "care, concern and attention." The word *heal* comes from the root meaning, "to make whole." The curing often comes from an external source: a pill, surgery, intervention, or procedure. The healing comes from within. It is absolutely possible that the two can exist exclusive of one another. Here's another example.

Another client came in with neck pain. Again, I wondered who was the pain in his neck. We discussed this briefly and I asked what else was happening with his body. He told me that he had blood in his urine. WAY beyond my scope of practice as a massage therapist. I asked the requisite questions. Have you seen your doctor? Is there any pain? Are you having any other symptoms? And he assured me that he was seeing his doctor in two days and he was probably just passing a kidney stone, he gets them all the time. (Ow!) I looked up some stuff in my symptom handbook, we talked for another second and I got him on the table. As I worked on his neck the following conversation ensued:

Me: So, blood in the urine huh?

Him: Yeah.

Me: So, anything you might be pissed off about?

Him: Oh…yeah, I get it…blood in the urine, pissed, yeah, I get it.

Me: So?

Him: Nope, nothing I'm pissed about. But I get it.

Me: Oh, ok, because I know you're frustrated with your job and would like things to be different there, so I didn't know if it escalated to pissed off.

Him: No, not pissed off.

Me: Ok

So I dropped it. And we were quiet for about three minutes until he started talking about his job. He told me how no one does their work and everyone is stupid and he couldn't wait to retire, but has three more years before his full pension, and why can't anyone do what they're supposed to? He wished he could leave now, but just can't and what is wrong with people. (I'm thinking, "Hmmm, he sounds kinda pissed off," but I just let him keep talking) and he ended the tirade with "But I'm not pissed off, I'm not pissed off…there's just this…this…series of little irritations."

I said, "Oh, like kidney stones?"

He laughed uncomfortably and sadly said, "Yeah."

And the conversation ended.

Well, it turned out that he didn't have kidney stones; he had bladder cancer. And he did the smartest thing he could have done. He quit his job. Three years early, with less pension and not as good health insurance. I fully believe had he not quit, his cancer would have come back. And I also believe had this been addressed more fully when it was just kidney stones that it might not have escalated to cancer. He went through the curing which the doctors provided, but he also went through the healing, which he did himself. To this day he remains cancer free.

See here's the thing about the mind and emotions. They don't like to be ignored or stuffed or diminished. If we don't acknowledge them they will have a tantrum like a child in the supermarket. It starts out with "mommy, mommy, mommy" and tugging on the skirt and soon, if ignored long enough, they will start ripping things off shelves. His kidney stones were mommy, mommy and the cancer was the tantrum. Now again, there are numerous causes for disease and please don't misunderstand; By no means am I saying that he <u>caused</u> his own cancer. I'm saying the stuffed emotions contributed. I am pointing out an observation; illness picks the area of vulnerability and expresses things that are previously unexpressed, typically after a bout of stress.

If we can't find a way to deal with our reactions to stress, it gives the same result. So, let's talk about the stress response.

The Stress Response

First off, what is stress? One of my favorite definitions is "A threat, real or imagined." Often it's something coming from the external world that we think we don't have the resources to deal with. It has a lot to do with feelings of powerlessness, hopelessness and helplessness. It has been observed throughout time that those three conditions lead to increased disease. From a physiological perspective it's a cascade of catecholamine hormones, such as adrenaline or noradrenalin, which facilitate immediate physical reactions associated with a preparation for violent muscular action. These include the following: [40]

-Acceleration of heart and lung action
-Paling or flushing, or alternating between both
-Inhibition of stomach and upper-intestinal action to the point where digestion slows down or stops
-General effect on the sphincters of the body
-Constriction of blood vessels in many parts of the body
-Liberation of nutrients (particularly fat and glucose) for muscular action
-Dilation of blood vessels for muscles
-Inhibition of the lacrimal gland (responsible for tear production) and salivation
-Dilation of pupil (mydriasis)
-Relaxation of bladder
-Inhibition of erection
-Auditory exclusion (loss of hearing)
-Tunnel vision (loss of peripheral vision)
-Disinhibition of spinal reflexes
-Shaking

---

[40] Henry Gleitman, Alan J. Fridlund and Daniel Reisberg (2004). Psychology (6 ed.). W. W. Norton & Company. ISBN 0-393-97767-6.

The fight-or-flight response (also called the fight-or-flight-or-freeze response, hyperarousal, or the acute stress response) was first described by Walter Bradford Cannon.[41],[42] the placebo researcher I mentioned previously.

His theory states that animals react to threats with a general discharge of the sympathetic nervous system, priming the animal for fighting or fleeing. This response was later recognized as the first stage of a general adaptation syndrome that regulates stress responses among vertebrates and other organisms.[43]

In the stress response, the immune system is at first heightened to help us fight any infection. But if we continue to operate in this heightened state of stress for prolonged periods of time, the immune system starts to weaken and disease can take hold of us. Historically, after the danger passed, hormone levels would decrease and we would sleep. Now with our stress at a constant level we don't get that break. This explains the all too common situation of a person who works under constant pressure to meet a deadline, and when she finally allows herself to go on vacation, she gets sick on the first day. Her body finally has a chance to rest and the virus can take hold.

A body under stress often has trouble with proper digestion, sleep, sexual function and nutrient absorption. This is why being in a constant agitated state is not only bad for our health but leads to more prescriptions and medical interventions.

---

[41] Some references say he first described the response in 1914 in The American Journal of Physiology. Others in the 1915 edition of *Bodily Changes in Pain, Hunger, Fear and Rage*. Other sources say that he first used the term in 1929 or in 1932 edition of the same book. The issue needs further research.

[42] Walter Bradford Cannon (1915). *Bodily Changes in Pain, Hunger, Fear and Rage: An Account of Recent Researches into the Function of Emotional Excitement*. Appleton-Century-Crofts.

[43] http://en.wikipedia.org/wiki/Fight-or-flight_response. Accessed November 5, 2011.

The opposite of this stress reaction is the Relaxation Response, coined by Dr. Herbert Benson, which calms the stress response and releases feel good hormones. Whereas the stress response is very helpful in warning us against immediate danger and getting us moving to react, our current stressors are not as dynamic. It's not a saber tooth tiger around the corner that eventually moves away so we can recover; it's the economy, the IRS, our spouse, job insecurities, our kids, our boss, and other daily stresses that don't seem to subside. These constant, low-grade stressors don't allow our body the natural downturn in the hormones followed by sleep. When we don't get a break from our reaction to stress it starts to manifest as problems in our bodies. Studies have shown that increasing the Relaxation Response not only slows heart and respiratory rate and decreases blood pressure but also slows the genetic expression of aging. That's right; relax more, age more slowly. Stress also affects our sleep cycle and brain function. This is why numerous experts from every facet of medicine estimate that 60-80% of our doctor's visits are due to stress-related disease. Some report as high at 90%. The same statistics are applied to workplace accidents.

Another aspect of stress is that our body can't distinguish between what we are imagining and what is happening external to ourselves. This is why we can have dreams during sleep that are so real, we wake up scared or mad or guilty that we slept with the paperboy. So in the same vein, by using our thoughts and fantasizing about something that's not really happening, we can cause a change in our physiology and stress levels. We are actually forming new connections in the brain constantly (called plasticity) and thinking something over and over can change the neural pathways. This is why imagining negative situations or worrying about things that aren't real can make our bodies react so negatively, and why creative visualization and affirmations work.

We have all had experiences where we get ourselves so worked up over something that we made ourselves sick.

This is why it is extremely important to only think positive, productive thoughts. We get enough stress from the outside; we don't need to be making up any more inside our heads. Now that we've talked about stress, let's see how dealing with this stress response can help you.

Helping Ourselves Deal with Stress

I was privileged enough to spend a week at The Benson-Henry Institute for Mind Body Medicine at Harvard Medical School. I joined about 120 medical doctors and other health professionals on a quest for understanding what stress does to us and how we can reverse the effects. We spent time meditating, doing cognitive restructuring, working with bio-dots, laughter therapy, yoga, chi gong and tai chi and learning about sleep, supplements and prescriptions. It was a truly life changing experience and I spoke with many physicians that said they were on their way home to make changes in their practice and convince their hospitals to adjust policies in how they treat patients. It was incredible!
So, here are a few life scenarios that might sound familiar to you and what Harvard taught me to do about it.

You have a busy day ahead and many things to do before you can relax with your massage appointment in the afternoon. Things get backed up because your son forgot his project and you have to take it to the school, traffic is crazy because of a water main break on the road, the post office only has one staff person and the lady in front of you has to look at every stamp ever printed before she finally decides on the flowers. You are rushed and hurried and frustrated. You snap at your husband on the phone and by the time you get on the massage table 10 minutes late you are even more stressed than before. What if you could learn a simple technique to help with relaxation all day long to keep your mind quiet and relaxed?

Scenario number two. We all have thoughts, about 60,000 a day actually. Often they are nice, pleasant thoughts but sometimes they are negative, self-defeating, self-limiting bad thoughts. Sometimes they sneak in when we don't want them there like during a class, when we're trying to read, sleep or even make love. Sometimes it's a stressful situation that is eating at us, keeping us awake at night and disturbing their thought process. What if there was a way we could deal with our daily stresses and repetitive thoughts and keep the mind on track?

Both of these folks could benefit from invoking the Relaxation Response. So, what types of things will help? Meditation, Yoga, tai chi, chi gong and breath work are some of the things that they could do for themselves, with no need for anyone else to help get them relaxed.

So let's say we can incorporate the Relaxation Response into scenario one. I learned a technique called "minis." These are mini meditations that take just a few minutes to do. And you can do them anywhere. There have been several times that I've taken a minute or two before my client goes in the treatment room to do a mini with them and get them relaxed before the massage or consultation. Because we can't control our stress, we CAN control our thoughts about the stress. I say to them, "Wow, client so-and-so, you seem a little stressed today, would it be okay if we started with some relaxation before the massage and just took a few minutes to help calm you?" They say sure. I have them sit comfortable in a chair and close their eyes. I ask them to concentrate on their breath either by paying attention to the rise and fall of their chest or the feeling of the air going in and out of the nostrils. And then use one of the following scripts:

Mini #1: Count very slowly to yourself from 10 down to 0, one number on each outbreath.
Breathe in, and on your first outbreath, say "10" to yourself.
With the next outbreath, say "9," working your way down to "0." When you get to "0," notice how you feel.

Mini #2: As you breathe in, count slowly up to "4;" as you breathe out, count slowly back down to "1."
As you breathe in, you say quietly to yourself, "1.. 2.. 3.. 4," and as breathe out, you say quietly to yourself, "4.. 3.. 2.. 1."
Do this several times.

Mini #3: This is counting the space between the inbreath and the outbreath.
After each inbreath, pause and count, "1.. 2.. 3;" after each outbreath, pause again and count, "1.. 2.. 3."
Do this several times.

Mini #4: Thich Nhat Hanh, a Vietnamese Buddhist, uses this as his favorite Mini.
On the inbreath, you think, "I am;" and on the outbreath, you think, "at peace." Repeat this several times.
This is also an excellent Mini to use while walking. And by the way, this also is my favorite mini, which I use often and teach at my workshops. Here is a link to be walked through it: http://youtu.be/N2nhSci40v0

Mini #5: Square breathing. Visualize a square. On the inbreath, visualize a vertical line and then a horizontal line. On the outbreath, you visualize another vertical and horizontal line and you complete the square.

(These are just a few mini's which I'm providing here compliments of Ann Webster at the Benson-Henry Institute for Mind Body Medicine.)

There you have it, just a short period of time to erase that detrimental stress response, calm the mind and enhance the body. I recommend minis to everyone and this technique can be great for children too; it's so easy to learn.

I use this technique when in traffic (don't close your eyes), a few times a day when I feel like I need a little break and sometimes even during a massage when the client is particularly quiet. I use that time to quiet my own mind and do the repetition of (inhale) I am, (exhale) at peace.

Now, for those of you who don't know me, let me explain a bit about me. I'm very type A. My husband describes me as type A+++++. I'm also competitive, anal retentive, a control freak, a Capricorn, an only child and the daughter of a dad that wanted a son. Oh, and if I can't win, I don't want to play. You can see that I have a lot going against me with this meditation thing. In the past, meditation teachers have told me to quiet my mind and I've laughed out loud. It just doesn't work. I think a lot and I think fast. I also talk and walk fast. So shutting off thoughts AND sitting still are big challenges for me. So…when I'm at Harvard and the instructor tells me we're going to meditate, I think, "Oh crap." But then she tells me the two rules of meditation.

1. Focus on something repetitive; your breath, a sound, a word, phrase or mantra.
2. If a thought comes through, just dismiss it without judgment and continue with what you were concentrating on.

Huh? It's that simple? No shutting off my mind, contorting my body or holding weird finger positions? Sure, you can do all those things. But the two rule system works for me. And I found, very quickly, that I could follow those two rules and intruding thoughts ceased, my body relaxed and I didn't want to stop. If I can do it….anyone can do it. Seriously! And remember this calms our bodies, enhances the immune system, balances our blood pressure, readies our brain for higher functioning and slows the genetic effect of aging. Why are we not doing this more?

Now, that covers our first scenario of daily stress. But what about the stressful, repetitive thoughts that are driving you crazy? My client with the fear of letting her children go or the woman with the neck issues from reliving her past? What can be done for them? I turn back to Harvard and want to teach you about cognitive restructuring.

Cognitive Restructuring. What Is It?

A cognitive-behavioral therapy technique used to identify and correct negative thinking patterns. The technique involves altering negative automatic thoughts that occur in anxiety-provoking situations (such as "They think I'm boring.") by replacing them with more rational beliefs (such as "I can't read other people's minds; they are probably just tired.") As thoughts are challenged and disputed, their ability to elicit anxiety is weakened.[44]

Here's the thing about stress. As I mentioned before, it's not so much the stress that's the problem; it's our reaction to it that is often exaggerated, distorted and irrational. We usually can't change the stress; it is something beyond our control, that's why we're stressed about it.

However, what we can change are our reactions and thoughts. These automatic reactions are often born out of negative programming. We may have had a negative experience in the past, all the way back to childhood, now we have an event that triggers that kneejerk reaction. Sometimes it's totally founded, but often isn't appropriate for the situation. By changing our thinking, we can decrease our reaction to the stress.

For example, if we had a parent who cheated in their marriage, we might be hypersensitive to that experience. So now, in our own marriage if we have a spouse that is late home from work one night, it might trigger an unconscious reaction that they are having an affair when in reality they are simply stuck in traffic or in a meeting with their boss. Imagine how many unpleasant arguments and stressful sleepless nights could be avoided if we could eliminate those automatic responses. Cognitive restructuring is a great

---

[44]http://socialanxietydisorder.about.com/od/glossary/g/restructuring.htm retrieved November 5, 2011.

technique for controlling unwanted thoughts and one that I have taught numerous clients. If this is something you think that you'd like to try, I do recommend learning more about this technique than what I mention here as I just give you the basics. I do include a blank chart on page 46. I'll use my own stressor as an example just for simplicity sake.

Across the top of the page, you list your stressor "I can't get my condo rented."

The first column is how the stressor makes you feel physically. It made me feel queasy, sleepless and made my heart race.

The second column is for emotions about the issue. From an emotional perspective I felt anxious, angry, fearful and humiliated.

Column three is for the repetitive thoughts you have surrounding the stressor. My repetitive thoughts were "I'll be broke," "I'll never get it rented," "We're stupid for buying the place at all," and more, with the distortions listed next to it (column four).

Column four are the distortions that those thoughts have (More about distortions on page 50).

Column five is how you would like to feel. In control, secure, in charge, taken care of, relaxed.

Then row six, though labeled positive thoughts are action items that you can do. It's the most important column.

Cognitive Restructuring Chart

Coping Key: Negative, Irrational Thoughts = Cognitive Restructuring
Negative, Rational Thoughts under my control = Problem Solving
Negative, Rational Thoughts I can't control = Acceptance (Find Meaning)

Stressful Event:

Physical Signs	Emotions	Automatic Thoughts	Cognitive Distortions	Positive Emotions	Positive Thoughts
List how you felt physically as a result of this stress.	List how you felt as a result of this stress.	Write the thoughts you recall having had as a result to this stress.	Identify the distortion(s) present in each unnecessarily negative thought.		

Physical Signs, Negative Emotions/Feelings, and Cognitive Distortions: All of these are generally the same no matter what your stress so they are your **"Stress Warning Signs."** Notice how your stress-related thoughts focus on what you **don't want.** As you think more positive thoughts, focus on what you **do want**.

Provided by Benson Henry Institute for Mind Body Medicine's Relaxation Response Resiliency Program (3RP) treatment manual.

As I reread all of what I had written, I realized how ridiculous it was. "I was going to be broke?" Really, all my money would be gone and I'd be living on the street? Really, is that true? No, of course not, but my distorted thinking made it seem that way. Another one... "We'll never get it rented." Really, it will sit empty until the day I die. No one, ever again, will rent that condo? Again, when you say it out loud and write it down, it seems ridiculous and what I realized was that it had only been available for two weeks. Not several months, not years, just two weeks.

The column of how I want to feel is pretty self-explanatory. It's the action steps in the last column, which are most important. I thought hard about what I could do to remedy the situation. Also, of course adding in that it had only been open for two weeks and we have always gotten it rented before. Those are two plusses! What else could we do aside from take a deep breath and do a mini? We could hire a rental agency, we could lower the rent, we could advertise in different places, accept Section 8 and if it really got that bad, we could try to sell the property.

Just knowing that there were actionable things I could do, decreased my stress about the situation. It gave me a modicum of control. Also, seeing how distorted my thinking was about the situation relieved a lot of the stress. Was the condo still for rent after I finished this process? Yes, but I could handle the stress in a rational way and deal better with the situation. We can't control our feelings, but we can control our <u>thoughts</u> about those feelings. You can do this with virtually any stressor you are having.

Once you learn how to fill out the simple chart and to identify the distortions, it's an easy technique that you can use for almost any repeat offender of stress. Again, this is much easier if someone facilitates it for you; seek out a qualified professional to help you through this experience.

Once I started using the chart on a few issues I now find that I don't even need to fill it out, it comes naturally to me. I don't have the immediate stressful kneejerk reaction to situations that before learning these techniques would have put me in a tailspin.

Another personal example: In 2010 the IRS audited my husband and me. For anyone that's gone through that, I'm so sorry. For those of you that haven't, lucky you! It was 8 weeks of stress, little sleep and crazy irrational thoughts. (I hadn't been to Harvard yet).

Fast forward to 2011. We actually got a tax refund that year. (You remember those, it's when you get money back.) I noticed that the state's had arrived, but the federal hadn't and I emailed Ernie, our tax guy, to check on it. He investigated and said that it came up on the computer as "Delayed." I began to panic. I emailed him back, "What the hell does delayed mean, is that bad?" He emailed back, "Well, in a word, yes. The only other times I've seen it delayed was when they didn't believe a deduction and wanted proof. Another time when someone's identity had been stolen and a fraudulent claim had already been filed. I'd call them this week."

With that I started to panic. This is BS. What did we do wrong? Is this going to happen to us every year? Why are they picking on us? I don't have the time to deal with this! And on and on. You can imagine.

Then I realized something. I realized that all I knew was the word "Delayed." It's not a scary word. "Delayed." I made the decision that I would just go with the concept that it was simply… "Delayed." Nothing was wrong, nothing had happened. Why was I going to freak out, stress out and lose sleep over a word? If I got a letter in the mail saying that something was wrong, then I would react. Because, I didn't know anything yet, I was having a reaction based on a past experience. To top it off, we had turned in a perfect tax return. Even if they disputed something, they would find nothing incorrect. I emailed Ernie telling him I was just going to assume that it was simply delayed and that I would wait. Six days later the money arrived in my bank account. It had simply been…delayed. Now, let's look at some of the distortions we can have. I was also taught these at Harvard and there are many phenomenal resources that list about 15 distortions. I'll discuss some below.

Cognitive Distortions

Distortions are exaggerated, irrational thoughts that cloud our responses to situations. We all tend to rely on our favorites and there is a great list of them in Dr. David Burns' book, *Feeling Good Handbook*. A few examples follow.

I have a friend who is an amazing artist. Once, many, many years ago, an art teacher told him he wasn't very good. He now won't show his work. This is distorted thinking and called a *mental filter*. Rather than focusing on all the positive things he's been told, he dwells on one comment from a mean man decades earlier. I've seen a lot of my actor friends suffering from this. Fabulous reviews suddenly mean nothing when one random person criticizes one aspect of one performance.

Another common one is called *magnification* where one little thing becomes a very serious thing. A pain in the side is surely cancer or a headache is a brain tumor. I hear things like this from my clients a lot and you can see how this would interfere with functioning.

And how many of us hear this, "I should be stretching, I should quit smoking, I should eat less carbs, I should call my mother, I should...." And the list is endless. These *should statements* are another distortion.

Jumping to conclusions involves two types of distortion, *mind reading* and *fortune telling*. Mind reading goes like this, "Hmmm, my husband is being really quiet today, I wonder if he is mad at me?" And then you dwell on that and build it up in your mind. And fortune telling is not asking the boss for a raise because you know you aren't going to get it anyway.

Another one I see very frequently with clients is *labeling and mislabeling*. These sentences start with "I'm a" or "he's a"...these tend to be belittling overly simplistic statements. "I'm a fat slob" or "I'm a loser because I ate 4 donuts at work."

And the last one I'll cover here (go get the whole list from Burn's book, they are great) is called *woe is me.* The world is out to get the person. This can be easy to fall into when you're in pain, but it soon becomes a way of life. Some of the others are *perfectionism, approval seeking* and *personalization.*

If we can identify our distortions and work with them using cognitive restructuring, we can decrease the stress response and function better.

BioDots

Biodots® are another tool that I was introduced to at Harvard. These are small stickers that you put on your hand and they read temperature to tell you when you are stressed.

The following is from the official Biodot website.

In the early 1970's Robert Grabhorn created the first ever Biodot skin thermometer. His original name for the product - Mood Mark. He quickly began working with leaders in the biofeedback and stress management industry. Soon the small, encapsulated crystals became known as the Biodot. The family business has since produced over 100 million of the Biodot skin thermometers, which have been sold in over 40 countries throughout the world.

Structurally, Biodot skin thermometers are small circles of micro-encapsulated liquid crystals of a thermal range, gauged to the variance of skin temperature. These remarkable space-age devices monitor skin temperature and change colors accordingly. When the person wearing the Biodot is stressed or feels stressful, he or she can make an effort to calm down.

What is so fun about these little stickers is that it gives you a visual cue when you are feeling stressed. If you're thinking, "Geez, it's pretty clear when I'm feeling stressed." I'll give you another personal example.

I had been introduced to the Biodots during day two at Harvard. We were told what they did, that they monitored temperature by changing color, (pretty and blue/purple for relaxed or warm and icky brown for cold or stressed) that breathing on them or putting them under your arm is cheating and that it's NOT a competition. For some reason the instructor looked at me to say that. We were also assured that our dot wasn't broken but inevitably at every class someone came up to them at lunch and expressed that they were given a broken dot. I put on my dot and all day long I watched it. It didn't budge off black (I was sure it was broken, but didn't want to say). It was very cold in the room so it made sense that it remained unchanged.

I had found a dance class to go to after class so I rushed back to the hotel, changed, caught a taxi and hurried over to Cambridge to take the class. About half way through class, my dot was changing color. It stopped at a nice blue color, but by the end of class, it was back to black. (The dots can only register temperatures that are so high and I was overheated) I was bummed! But by the time I left class and got back in the taxi that post-exercise relaxed-feeling kicked in and I looked at my dot and it was changing color again. I was so excited. By the time I got back to the hotel, it was a gorgeous purple color. I was able to sustain this color through dinner, a shower (with my hand outside the curtain) and while watching some TV.

Then I decided to call my husband who was home in California. He asked how my day was and I proudly told him that my dot was purple. He simply said uh huh. (He's used to things like that coming out of my mouth.) He started to explain to me that the cat was sick and he was really worried. As he got more and more hyper about the cat, I could see that my dot was starting to fade. By the end of the conversation, he had worked himself into quite a state about the cat and was getting very upset. No matter how hard I tried to stay calm during the conversation, my dot was getting darker and darker until it was a very unpleasant pea color. I finally told him that I had to get off the phone because he was making my dot black. He still had no idea what that meant but figured it was significant so we ended the conversation. I looked at my poor dot. It looked terrible.

So I sat on the edge of the bed and did a mini and concentrated on my breath for just a few minutes. When I opened my eyes, my dot was purple again. What this illustrated to me was how just a little amount of stress actually affects us. I didn't feel particularly upset talking with my husband but clearly on some level I was affected. It also wasn't a horribly stressful situation, but nevertheless my body reacted quickly. You can imagine what a truly stressful situation would do. It was also phenomenal to see how quickly I could regain the Relaxation Response by doing a mini and taking a few deep breaths. I was able to completely undo the stress that was caused by the phone conversation. It was remarkable and you can do it too.

I purchased a large supply of Biodots and I give them to clients and hand them out during lectures. To me, it is a simple and effective way to illustrate the stress that we feel in our bodies and might not even be aware of. More information can be found at http://www.biodots.net.

And if you leave me a review of this book on Amazon and email me to tell me you did so, I will send you your very own biodots. drkathygruver@gmail.com Put the word biodots in the subject line.

When Nothing is Everything. The Placebo

I introduced the relevance of the placebo effect in the chapters on mind/body medicine. This chapter expands on that. It is so much more than a phenomenon that annoys pharmaceutical companies. These days, a drug is not considered legitimate unless a double blind randomized placebo-controlled study has been undertaken. With more research showing that the placebo itself can be a treatment, even those types of studies might not be worth the paper they are printed on.

As I mentioned earlier, the placebo started to get major attention when Beecher introduced a study called *The Powerful Placebo*. His study showed that about 35% of the population was susceptible to this phenomenon. Though his study has been criticized for many reasons over the years, we cannot escape the fact that the placebo is real and it works for many people. The placebo effect is difficult to prove. We see that we can program our physiology with our words as a means of changing expectations and outcomes. We can also illustrate the placebo effect with fake drugs and procedures. The question is how, when, why and on whom will it work? These are questions yet to be definitively answered, but I say, if it might work…let's use it!

I can help program the outcomes of my treatments, by saying that it will help, that my clients look straighter, or that his or her shoulder has loosened up. I would rather program my clients with that expectation, than "Wow, this isn't doing a thing." Or "Gee, you're just as stiff as you were when you came in." Those types of phrases don't help and I've heard practitioners say such things.

The esthetician I go to for facials says the same thing after every treatment I have with her, "Wow, your skin looks fabulous, you are just glowing!" If she doesn't say it to me, then her receptionist does. Is my skin glowing? Maybe,

maybe not. But they have just programmed me to feel fabulous about how I look.

One of the big questions is how do we test the placebo in an ethical way? Sham knee surgery certainly did seem to be effective, but we can't go around tricking people into having surgeries. Dr. Benedetti, a researcher out of the University of Turin in Italy has done numerous studies on the placebo by using open vs. hidden treatment and has written books about the research. In this method, the placebo and/or real medication is either given directly to the patient and told it is a drug, or completely hidden from view so that the patient doesn't know that anything is happening. The results have been startling. Using hidden vs. open treatments seems to be the future of research to show just what power the placebo has for healing.

Here are my summaries of studies illustrating what the placebo can do. (If technical studies aren't your thing, feel free to skip over them to the next section.)

In a study by Wager,[45] using functional magnetic resonance imaging (fMRI), it was shown that a placebo stimulates areas in the brain that respond to pain. In one study, researchers were able to decrease the amount of pain by 22%, with 72% of the participants showing a rate of decreased pain using just a placebo. This indicates a belief in the treatment by the majority of participants. These findings show that the placebo effect has a physical effect and is more than simply report bias. Their findings also show evidence for expectation-induced placebo effects with opioid-containing regions in the mid-brain active during anticipation. This study proves that pain is not only a physical sensation, but can be affected psychologically.

---

[45] Wager, T., Rilling, J., Smith, E., Sokolik, A., et al. (2004). Placebo-Induced Changes of fMRI in the Anticipation and Experience of Pain. *Science*, *303*(5661), 1162-1167.

Scientists are using brain imagery to compare pain responses and placebo responses. This type of study is illustrated in an article by Petrovic.[46] Researchers compared analgesic effects of a placebo treatment and a rapid acting opioid. They found that both treatments stimulated various parts of the brain. Participants noted that the placebo decreased their pain response, which was explained by the researchers that they had been informed and believed that the placebo was actually a powerful pain reducer. This response was diminished by the opioid antagonist naloxone and appears to be opioid dependent. The conclusion of this study is that the placebo effect goes deeper than just the subjective thoughts of the patient; it actually causes notable changes in the brain.

In another study, Hrobjartsson[47] questions whether the placebo is actually as powerless as many scientists intimate. He examined 114 previously conducted studies to chart the outcomes of placebo studies. He found the typical placebo to be a lactose tablet or a machine that was used while turned off. These studies showed successful placebo response for pain reduction, lowered diastolic blood pressure, decrease in time to fall asleep, and weight loss. On the other hand he did note that most successful placebo studies have been done on small groups of people and postulates that perhaps unsuccessful trials are not published. He also acknowledges that the placebo effect could be attributed to poor methodology in small trials. In his assessment, there was no significant evidence that placebos in general have powerful clinical effects. He noted no noteworthy effect on subjective or objective binary or continuous objective outcomes. He, at this time, cannot recommend placebo for anything outside of

[46] Petrovic, P., Kalso, E., Petersson, K., Ingvar, M. (2002). Placebo and opioid analgesia-Imaging a shared neuronal network. *Science*, 295, 1737-1740. 17 October 2001; accepted 23 January 2002. Published online 7 February 2002. 10.1126/science.106176.

[47] Hrobjartsson, A., Gotzsche, P. (2001). Is the placebo powerless? *The New England Journal of Medicine, 344*(21), 1594-1603.

a controlled clinical trial. (I included this study to illustrate that even though evidence is mounting for a clinic use for the placebo, there are still those experts that refute it.)

What is the placebo effect and what is the best way to test for it, questions Benedetti[48] in his recent study of placebo analgesia. There are so many mechanisms underlying the placebo response; expectation, conditioning, regression to the mean or a patient trying to please the physician. He proposes that the best way to measure placebo is to have a complete non-treatment group. But how to do that blind? The key is open vs. hidden treatment. This takes away the anticipation, expectation, and verbal cues. His research shows that proven pain medication like morphine and tramadol are significantly less effective when given through hidden injection than open ones when the patient expects the pain to decrease. This strongly illustrates the link between the patients' perspective and is a new method of illustrating the placebo effect.

When the patient is unaware that a treatment is being administered, the treatment is less effective.[49] If the drug is really effective, symptom reduction should occur with distribution of the medication, whether hidden or open. The following example clearly illustrates this point. A doctor gave a patient a powerful pain medication and told them their pain would subside in moments. In contrast, another patient was given a dose of powerful pain medication from a hidden machine. They found that the dose needed to reduce pain by 50% was much higher with the hidden dosing than with the open dose. During the first hour post-surgery, pain ratings were much higher with hidden dosing than with open

[48] Benedetti, F. (2006). Placebo Analgesia. *Neurological Science*, 27, S100-S102.

[49] Colloca, L., Lopiano, L., Lanotte, M., Benedetti, F. (2004). Overt versus covert treatment for pain, anxiety and Parkinson's disease. *The Lancet Neurology*, 3(11), 679-684.

dosing. Similarly, patients had a faster relapse when they were told a medication was being stopped as opposed to it being concluded without their knowledge. The fear of pain might have a hyperalgesic effect acting as a nocebo. A similar trial was conducted adjusting their brain stimulators of Parkinson's patients. When the stimulus was adjusted (lowered) with the explanation that their symptoms would worsen, they did. When the stimulus was lowered covertly, no change in function was observed. They conclude that the awareness of the treatment, presence of the therapist and expectation of outcome are clinically relevant. Secondly, when the treatment must be interrupted, it is more beneficial for the patient not to know. The researchers believe that more investigation involving open vs. hidden treatment will improve the understanding of the placebo and how it can be used effectively in treatment.

Affirmations, The Power of Words

In learning to change our minds, I've found one of the simplest and most effective techniques is using affirmations. Some experts estimate that we have around 60,000 thoughts a day and that 50,000 of those are negative. That's 80% negative thoughts, which translates to me as 80% negative results. It's so easy, especially with what's happening in the world today to let our thoughts go to fear, worry and fatalism. And it is important to acknowledge our feelings and note that we do have fear and concern, but when these thoughts start to rule our minds and become repetitive and distorted as we talked about in the previous chapters, it can lead to illness and negative changes in our bodies.

Add to this that 60-80% of visits to the doctor are caused by stress. If we look at our life at this exact second, where is the stress? Seriously, look at this moment in time. What is wrong? Our thoughts, and thus our stress, are often in the future and usually about something that we're not even sure is going to happen. We talk about it, think about it and dwell on it even if it's not guaranteed. Like we learned before, we can't control our emotions, but we can control our thoughts. I'll teach you another way to do that. We've talked about emotion/body correspondence, cognitive restructuring, mini meditations and the stress response. The next technique is affirmations, using positive language to program our lives.

I find this especially useful when negative thoughts interfere with our ability to fall asleep. Try repeating the following phrase, "I fall asleep quickly and easily, I wake up feeling refreshed." These types of short phrases do one of two things. Either, they program you to fall asleep quickly and wake up feeling refreshed or, at the very least, it shuts out the other thoughts that are running through your head. There is a physics axiom that states "Two solid objects cannot occupy the same space at the same time." The same principle applies with our thoughts. We can't be thinking two things at once. That's what counting sheep is all about; it distracts us from those repetitive thoughts that plague us at bedtime. I'm not saying changing our thoughts and words is easy. On the contrary, it can be quite hard at first. Especially if we have been programmed to think negatively since we were young or are surrounded by negativity in our lives. But it can be done with a little practice and the results are phenomenal.

When working with affirmations there are a few rules of thumb.

Make them short.
Keep them in the present tense.
Make them positive.
And repeat often!

So don't say, "I'm not sick anymore." Rephrase your wording to, "I am healthy and well." Saying, "I want to be rich," puts the emphasis on the future and focuses on a current state of lack. Saying, "I am wealthy and abundant," or "Money flows easily to me from unexpected sources," creates a positive present-time scenario.

So you can see that affirmations can do more than just attract good health. Here are some more examples.

I am wealthy and prosperous.
I am healthy and well.
My body is strong and resilient.
The universe provides for me.
I am divinely protected.
I attract love and support.
Supportive, helpful friends surround me.

I could go on and on. The most important thing is to recognize situations where you tend towards negativity and decide to change your mind. Going in to situations with a negative attitude doesn't benefit anyone and just makes life more unpleasant.

It's easy to incorporate affirmations into your life. Take some time to work these into your day by saying that at a certain set time or keeping them posted on your mirror, car dashboard or desktop. This is especially important if you are prone to negative thinking about your body or certain situations. Changing the speech from, "My neck always hurts," to "My neck is strong and healthy," can start to induce physiological changes. Once affirmations become part of your life, you'll be more in tune with when your thinking and words has become negative. If you'd like help have a friend or loved one <u>gently</u> remind you when you get off track.

Similar to affirmations is setting intentions. My Reiki Master, Diane Vaughn, always set intentions before the Reiki attunements that she provided. I didn't really understand it back then, but now I am a believer in their importance. Often, when we set an intention for something, it becomes easier to achieve. She used to phrase them this way:

My intention is to co-create with the universe, true healing for my body, mind and spirit. (Or whatever it is you are trying to achieve.)

She always started intentions, no matter what it was, with "co-create with the universe." Then she wrote them down for me and asked me to repeat them throughout my day.

It only takes a few moments to do the intention process. Take note what areas you would like to change and create (co-create) and design phrases that are empowering rather than limiting. The more we can expand our beliefs and consciousness, the more our worlds will expand with them.

For those of you who are interested in research on these topics, a few studies follow that I found during the work on my dissertation. These are my summaries of those studies.

Twenty-four participants took part in a study by Tod[50] marking the effect of out-loud self-instruction on the vertical jump. They were divided into four groups: motivational self-talk (I can jump high), instructional self-talk (bend and dive), neutral self-talk (count backwards from 1000 by 7's) and no instruction. Motivational self-talk is used to increase confidence, effort and energy by creating a positive mood (cited in Theodorakis, 2000). Instructional self-talk is used to trigger correct movement through focus, technique and strategy execution (cited in Theodorakis, 2000). Both instructional and motivational self-talk showed influence on higher center of mass displacement, greater impulse and quicker angular rotation of the knee compared with the neutral condition. Self-talk may have influenced cerebral cortex functioning, resulting in adjustments in motor unit recruitment, synchronization, firing rate or muscle contractility. Current findings reveal that self-talk influences muscular power. This could be used in the future to not only enhance sports performance, but to help with rehab in muscle injuries.

(This amazing study is one of my favorites. I was blown away by these results.)

In a study by Xu[51] the effect of mind power was tested on HIV-1 virus. The HIV virus was extracted and placed in a plate; researchers were trained to use visualization in an attempt to influence the structure of the virus. One group concentrated on "inhibit growth,", one "increase growth" and the other was the control. At the end of the experiment, the HIV that had been infused with the thoughts "increase" had increased more than the placebo and in the same vein, the

---

[50] Tod, D., Thatcher, R., McGuigan, M., Thatcher, J. (2009). Effects of instructional and motivational-talk on the vertical jump. *Journal of Strength and Conditioning Research, 23* (1), 196-203.

[51] Xu, J., & He, B. (2007). The effect of mind power on HIV-1: A pilot study. *Alternative Therapies in Health and Medicine, 13*(5), 40-2.

"inhibit" dish showed less HIV than the control. The results of this study point out that the human mind has the power to influence HIV growth and infectivity. This indicates that people can influence a virus, even outside of the body.

Raalte tested the effect of positive and negative self-talk on dart throwing performance.[52] Fifteen participants were asked to try to hit a bull's eye on a dartboard. They were divided into three groups: positive self-talk (you can do it), negative (you cannot do it) or neutral who said nothing. The positive talkers performed significantly better than their negative counterparts and the control subjects. The control group and negative talk group did not differ at all in throwing accuracy. As far as future expectations, the negative group stated that they expected to improve significantly more on future dart throwing than the positive or neutral condition subjects. This indicates that negative self-talk might be a motivating factor for future performance. It is clear however, that initial performance was better when positive self-talk was used.

Amigo[53] sought to find if verbal instructions could change blood pressure and heart rate in patients. The blood pressure of 120 subjects was studied, 60 hypertensive (high blood pressure) and 60 normotensive (normal blood pressure). Each of the 60 samples was randomly divided into four groups. Each subject was left alone in a room for five minutes. The researcher then measured the blood pressure and heart rate of each participant. Following this, each person was told that his or her blood pressure would increase, decrease or not change at all. The control group was given no instructions. Those who were told their

---

[52] Raalte, V., Brewer, J., Lewis, B., Linder, B., Darwyn, E. et al. (1995). Cork! The effects of positive and negative self-talk on dart throwing performance. *Journal of Sport Behavior, 18* (1), 50.

[53] Amigo, I., Cuesta, V., Fernandez, A., Gonzalez, A. (1993). The effect of verbal instructions on blood pressure measurement. *Journal of Hypertension, 11*(33), 293-296.

pressure would increase experienced a raise of 4.3 mmHg and 2.5 mmHg (normotensive and hypertensive respectively). Those who were told their blood pressure would decrease experienced a drop of 7.8 and 7.4 respectively. Those who were told no change would occur saw a drop of 3.5 and 1.8 respectively and the control group decreased by 5.6 and 4.2 respectively. These results show that verbal instruction does have an influence on blood pressure variation and more studies need to be conducted in this area.

Creative Visualization, Using Your Imagination for Health

Creative visualization or guided imagery is another amazing tool that you can easily incorporate into your life. I think most of us do it without even realizing it. Don't we visualize on a daily basis anyway, every time we daydream or fantasize?

One of the common visualization exercises involves seeing so clearly in your mind that you are eating a lemon that your mouth starts to water and you can taste the sourness.

I first learned about visualization when I was working on a community theatre production of *Oklahoma*. During a break in rehearsal an older Chinese man was showing tricks with playing cards. I mentioned to him that I thought I was getting sick because my throat was starting to hurt. He asked if I ever did visualization. (I was sixteen, what did I know?) I told him I didn't think so.

He explained to me that when he is starting to feel like he is coming down with something he activates his immune system by visualizing it. He pictures the white blood cells swarming to an area like the cavalry coming over the hill to save the day. He would lie quietly in bed and just imagine these creatures rushing to help. And often he would feel better and not get sick. And he said that kind of visualization could help with anything. I tried it that night, visualizing my white blood cells rushing to my throat to help and white light filling my neck. I woke up the next day pain free and didn't get sick. And I was brilliant as chorus girl number three in Oklahoma.

I used this technique for much more important things as my life went on. Since I'm big on personal examples, here's a good one.

I was a freshman in college, auditioning to be a dancer on a cruise ship. (I don't know, seemed like a good idea at the time.) I was warming up and kicking very high over my head when my other foot came out from underneath me and I fell right on my tailbone. (For those of you that felt that and made a face, make sure you read the section on being an empath).

Anyway, I got off the floor and just kept warming up and then proceeded to dance for a few hours. Later, I felt severe pain. I couldn't stand or sit for any period of time. I went to the doctor Monday who informed me after an x-ray that I had cracked a vertebra and they weren't sure how serious it was yet, but wanted to do some more tests. I was then scheduled for a 360° bone scan and told I might need to wear a back brace for six months. That did not make me happy.

This was where visualization came in. Every night I would picture that x-ray of my spine and picture the vertebrae and a little man dressed like a construction worker would show up and use his caulking gun to fill in the crack. He looked like the guy from Super Mario Bros™. I saw my white blood cells rushing there too and then also pictured warm, healing light. I did this every night with my hands on my low back.

I noticed the pain had subsided, but still needed Tylenol and ice occasionally. It also seemed that I had more range of motion and could sit longer. I returned to the doctor for my bone scan. Two days after the procedure I sat in his office dreading the news that I would need to be confined to a brace. He put the x-ray up on the light screen and next to it the bone scan. He counted down the vertebrae in the x-ray and said, "See, here is the crack." He then pointed to the bone scan "and you can see the crack here…" and then he stopped. He double checked the name on the x-ray and counted the vertebrae in both images. They both were mine and the images were identical. With one exception, the crack was gone. My dad looked at me. The doctor looked at me and said, "I don't know what you did kid, but you just saved yourself six months of discomfort," and I went home. It took a bit longer for the pain to be totally gone and I will admit that it is still a weak area in my body. Too much dancing or a bad mattress and I'll feel it, but this remarkable experience made me realize what the power of the mind could do to the body.

I have worked with cancer sufferers who use this type of visualizing. Whether they picture angels coming to take away the tumor, or bugs slowly eating it away, it has been proven to help our bodies heal. It is important to let the clients come up with an image that works for them. I read a story about a woman in a cancer support group where they were visualizing the body attacking the cancer and doing battle with it. One woman in the class was having no results and was actually starting to have anxiety over the experience. It turned out she witnessed much war when she was a child and found those images offensive and not healing. When she was allowed to pick her own non-violent visuals, she started to see great results.

We can also use external visual cues to help assist us. I had a client visualize what her uterine fibroids looked like. She ended up seeing a grey lump of clay. So I advised her to go to the art store, buy clay, make a fibroid and everyday as she did her visualization, to not only picture it getting smaller, but to take a chunk out of her clay fibroid as well. Now, as a note, if you are doing something like this, you might want to tell your family. Because unbeknownst to her, her son accidently grabbed her clay fibroid and used it for a school art project.

You can see how this type of imagery might be useful for healing. I had a lovely client who was dying of cancer. She was suffering greatly, in tremendous amounts of pain. During her sessions with me as I did Reiki we did a visualization. She was very big into angels and she was one herself. You could practically see them around her. We would do a visualization where angels were swooping in and carrying away her tumor. She was already terminal so we knew this wasn't going to "cure" her, but it provided her with a few things. 1. It decreased her pain and 2. It gave her a sense of control of her own life and illness. She passed soon after we started the visualizations, but it gave her much peace and healing on her journey.

Guided imagery can be simple, but also be quite involved. Some examples include someone leading you through imaginary lands and connecting with spirit guides, inner wisdom, etc. Here is a script for a guided journey to meet your spirit guide. Take your time as you read it aloud and allow pauses in the script to visualize.

Get into a comfortable position and let your eyes close. Concentrate on your breath, not trying to change it, just observing it. As your body relaxes further, see if you can detect any tension that is residing in your body. And let it go free. Now see yourself in a forest. Green and lush and verdant. There is slight moisture in the air and the birds are singing. Walk through the woods observing what is around you. Imagine that the deeper you walk into the forest, the more relaxed you become. Realize that your tension is melting away like the dew. See the light coming through the trees and sparkling on the leaves. Now, you come to a clearing in the woods and in the center are two logs to sit on. Choose one and sit down with your hands open on your lap. Look around you. Notice the trees, the rocks, the grass, and other natural things that make the clearing real for you. Now, coming out of the woods to sit across from you is your guide. See them approaching you and invite them to sit on the log opposite to you. After they sit, look into their eyes and see what they look like, a man or woman or something else? What are they wearing? What do their hands look like, how are they dressed? Ask them what their name is. Note their answer. Now sit with them and just be in their presence. Sit silently as long as you'd like and then see if they have any information for you. Or, ask them a question that you'd like an answer to and wait for the answer. Note what they say and do. Perhaps they speak, nod or gesture. Ask them how best to connect with them in the future knowing that they are a part of you and you can connect with them at any time. When your time together is over, thank them and turn to leave the woods. As you walk out of the forest let the message sink in and remain relaxed as you get back to the spot where you entered. Remain in this calm state as long as you'd like and then open your eyes and return to the present.

More information can be found at Academy for Guided Imagery at http://acadgi.com.

And here are some summaries of studies regarding guided imagery from my dissertation.

Sixty-eight adults with asthma were chosen by Epstein[54] (2004) and given instruction on guided imagery to help their asthma symptoms. Though the study did not indicate significant change in coughing, wheezing, activity, sleep or adverse events, a significant amount (47%) in the visualization group were able to decrease or discontinue their medication. The effect of imagery is often experienced for immediate symptom relief during an attack or impending attack. The researchers felt optimistic that by increasing the personal power of the sufferers they could feel more safe and secure and have more control over their illness. They deemed visualization to be a cost-effective addition to current asthma treatments; being inexpensive, safe and easily used for self-treatment among asthma sufferers. Though they did have some concerns from the current study, they hope that it precipitates interest in doing a larger, future study on how visualization can benefit asthmatics.

In another study, forty-four adults were observed to determine if guided imagery could have an effect on post-

---

[54] Epstein, G., Halper, J., Manhart Barrett, E., Birdsall, C., & et al. (2004). A pilot study of mind-body changes in adults with asthma who practice mental imagery. *Alternative Therapies in Health and Medicine, 10*(4), 66-71.

operative outcomes on same-day surgical procedures[55]. Preoperatively, the guided imagery group listened to a 28 minute CD where the control group had 28 minutes alone, but with no intervention. The guided imagery group had a significant decrease in mean anxiety levels from an initial 25.32 to a level of 11.86 after listening to the pre-op CD. No significant difference was reported for narcotic use, though the guided imagery group did use slightly less. There was also a marked difference in pain ratings at one hour, with the control group at 41.8 and the imagery group at 26.68 (measured on the Mann-Whitney U test). Pain levels for the imagery group at two hours were significantly lower than the control, 20.00 and 34.72 respectively. There was also a 9-minute difference in the length of stay in APU (ambulatory procedure unit) with the control group needing more time. In conclusion, this study illustrated that guided imagery shows promise to decrease anxiety, lower post-operative pain levels and shorten length of stay in the PACO (postoperative anesthesia care unit), even with a short period of time using the imagery CDs.

Bonadies[56] examines the role of guided imagery in pain and anxiety reduction in a study on children and post-operative pain.[57] Seventy three children about to undergo adenoid or tonsil surgery were divided into a control group, an intervention group consisting of video tape imagery, 30-minute audio tape a week before surgery, 1-4 hours after surgery and 22-27 hours after discharge. Children in the

---

[55] Gonzales, E., Ledesma, R., McAllister, D., Perry, S., Dyer, C., Maye, J. (2010). Effects of guided imagery on postoperative outcomes in patients undergoing same-day surgical procedures: A randomized, single-blind study. *AANA Journal, 78*(3), 181-188.

[56] Bonadies, V. (2009). Guided imagery as a therapeutic recreation modality to reduce pain and anxiety. *Therapeutic Recreation Journal, 43*(2), 43-55.

[57] Huth, M., Broome, M, Good, M. (2004). Imagery reduces children's post-operative pain. *Pain, 110*(1-2), 439-448. As cited by Bonadies (2009).

intervention group reported significantly less pain and anxiety after listening to the audiotape immediately after surgery: 28.3% less sensory pain, 10.5% less anxiety and 8.5% less affective pain. Though not statistically significant, once home, there was still less pain and anxiety.

Another study[58] demonstrated that relaxation with guided imagery (RGI) assisted with the stress response and wound healing in patients about to undergo cholecystectomy (gall bladder removal). The RGI group demonstrated less anxiety, lower cortisol one day post-op, and less surgical wound erythema (redness) than the control group.

Bonades[59] discusses a case study. A 52-year-old Hispanic male, with a diagnosis of AIDS, poly substance abuse and depression, complained of back pain, which was affecting his ability to walk. He agreed to try an imagery session. His pain reported pre-session was 8 out of 10. He seemed distraught and in despair regarding his pain. During the imagery session, the practitioner suggested he control his pain like you would an electric blanket, with a dial showing numbers that could be adjusted and progressive muscle relaxation was also incorporated. At the end of the 20-minute session the patient reported "a lot less pain" and stated the number was now 4 out of 10, decreased from eight. He participated in three follow up sessions and learned to control his pain on his own using a recorded tape or self-guided imagery. Guided imagery is an easy and inexpensive way to empower clients and see improvement in pain, anxiety and quality of life.

---

[58] Holden-Lund (1988). Effects of relaxation with guided imagery on surgical stress and wound healing. *Research in Nursing and Health, 11*(4), 235-44. (As cited by Bonadies, 2009).

[59] Bonadies, V. (2009). Guided imagery as a therapeutic recreation modality to reduce pain and anxiety. *Therapeutic Recreation Journal, 43*(2), 43-55.

Ball[60] studied the use of guided imagery for recurrent abdominal pain in children. Ten children were included in the study. They were trained in four weekly, 50-minute sessions of relaxation and guided imagery. They completed pain diaries at zero, one and two months and both the children and their guardians completed psychological questionnaires. The children experienced 67% decrease in pain over the course of the study, even though they were unresponsive to the conventional treatment provided by their physician and pediatric gastroenterologist. Guided imagery was judged to be an effective and safe treatment for childhood recurrent abdominal pain. I was only able to locate the abstract (summary) of this study.

Twenty-nine health volunteers were studied to see if guided imagery would have an effect on forearm blood flow.[61] Cutaneous blood flow and arm temperature were measured before conducting the study. All subjects were played a tape-recorded induction and relaxation script, which focused on regular breathing and relaxation. They also heard a script instructing "hot" and "cold" conditions. The "hot" script had the subject imagine the target arm near a fireplace and the "cold" script consisted of dipping the arm in icy water. Both scripts then asked the arms to return to normal. There was a marked decrease in temperature of the "cold" arm and a modest increase in the "hot" arm following presentation of the relevant script. For each measurement of blood flow, the flow was greater in the "hot" arm and less in the "cold" arm, compared to the control limb. This indicates that the reason for increase in heat was an increase in blood flow. For the "cold" arm, it seems that the blood flow did decrease in the

---

[60] Ball, T., Shapiro, D., Monheim, C., Weydert, J. (2003). A pilot study of the use of guided imagery for the treatment of recurrent abdominal pain in children. *Clinical Pediatrics, 42*(6), 527-532.

[61] McGuirk, J., Fitzgerald, D., Friedmann, P., Oakley, D., Salmon, P. (1998). The effect of guided imagery in a hypnotic context on forearm blood flow. *Contemporary Hypnosis, 15*(2), 101-108.

"cold" arm, but there was a significant increase in blood flow in the control arm. The outcome was affected by whether the left or right arm was targeted first. As with the temperature change, the blood flow change was more pronounced in the "cold" script. These results are encouraging evidence that this type of technique might be useful for leg ulcer patients and circulation issues.

Antall[62] investigated whether guided imagery would have an effect on pain and anxiety in older patients undergoing joint replacement surgery. Thirteen patients received either a music audiotape and conventional care and the other only a guided imagery audiotape. Pain medications prescribed for joint replacement patients can cause unwanted side effects such as confusion, falls and urinary incontinence. The average length of time in the acute setting is 3-5 days. The goal of this study was to challenge the effect of guided imagery on those two components. Patients were instructed to keep a journal of their experiences; the control group was to note their feelings and pain ratings, and the intervention group, their feelings, pain ratings and frequency of using the tapes. At the conclusion of the study there was a marked difference between the two groups. Pain ratings for the control group was 5.3 compared to 2.35 for the intervention group. The average length of hospital stay was 5.5 days shorter for the intervention group and use of morphine was almost halved for the imagery group. There was also a great decrease in anxiety from the baseline to day three. The use of guided imagery is clearly demonstrated here as being beneficial for numerous aspects of patient care. It is affordable, self-directed and effective. A broader study with a larger population is suggested.

---

[62] Antall, G., Kresevic, D. (2004). The use of guided imagery to manage pain in an elderly orthopaedic population. *Orthopaedic Nursing, 23*(5), 335-340.

Hypnosis: You are Getting Healthy

Hypnosis is another area of mind/body medicine that might benefit you. Hypnosis is very similar to guided imagery, with people achieving a relaxed state and then receiving suggestions on things to change. This is often very useful with behaviors such as smoking and over-eating. There is specific course of study for this system of medicine and it is recommended that you seek out a trained practitioner. Another option is to use pre-recorded audiotapes with hypnotic suggestions on it. These are available from numerous sources and can be played in the comfort of your own home. To me, hypnosis and creative visualization are similar, but there is an important difference. Typically visualization comes from inside you whereas hypnosis is led by someone else for the purpose of changing something like a habit or other repetitive condition. Here is a great definition of hypnosis.

Hypnosis: *A heightened state of suggestibility, such that the suggestions given are accepted as being true and effect the beliefs, habits, perceptions and behaviors of an individual in varying degrees according to the depth of hypnosis established. "Deeper levels" of hypnosis enable the hypnotized individual to experience greater hypnotic phenomenon such as light states being able to create catalepsy by suggestion, and deeper states allowing the individual to experience amnesia, anesthesia, and hallucinations. Generally there are several types of hypnosis, (1) naturally occurring hypnosis, (2) hetero hypnosis, (3) self-hypnosis, and (4) waking suggestion, which is similar to placebo.* Definition by Cal Banyan.[63]

There is a great article at Livestrong on the difference between guided imagery and hypnosis at the following site:

---

[63] Retrieved from http://www.hypnosis.org/free-hypnosis/hypnosis-information/definition-of-hypnosis.php November 20, 2011.

76

http://www.livestrong.com/article/152895-guided-imagery-vs-hypnosis/.

Peter Wright, a hypnotherapist in Santa Barbara says, "I believe hypnosis to be much more powerful than guided imagery because it can bring about rapid changes in the client since it can focus in particular on whatever the issue might be and -- using imagery -- help release/let go/empower the client to make different choices in their life."

Here are some studies on the benefits of hypnosis from my dissertation.

Ginandes[64] sought to discover if hypnosis could accelerate the healing of bone fractures. All eleven patients received standard orthopedic care and the study group underwent hypnotic intervention consisting of six individual sessions and audiotapes for daily home use, designed to augment fracture healing. The researchers hoped to prove that hypnosis could not only be used for functional healing, but also anatomical, structural healing. The radiologists' assessment showed faster healing of the hypnosis subjects through the ninth week. The significance occurred at week six for fracture edge, which resembled more closely the healing expected at week 8½. Until week twelve, the hypnosis group showed overall faster healing though both groups reaching their expected healing at that same time. The self-assessment of pain showed less pain for the hypnosis group overall and less use of analgesics. Hypnosis subjects reported more tenderness at week nine. For the functional testing, hypnosis patients had better plantar flexion and more mobility at week nine than the controls. The most frequently noted comments from hypnosis participants were greater pain reduction, more positive attitude, stress reduction, lowered anxiety and enhanced sense of relaxation. The findings that both radiological

[64] Ginandes, C., Rosenthal, D. (1999). Using hypnosis to accelerate the healing of bone fractures: A randomized controlled pilot study. *Alternative Therapies, 5*(2), 67-75.

measures (fracture line and edge) trended toward faster healing with hypnosis through the ninth week with a significant difference at week six, supports the researchers hypothesis that hypnosis can cause physiological changes in healing. The fact that both groups ended up with the same level of healing by the end of the trial indicates that perhaps hypnosis is more effective in early stages of healing. The hypnosis group did show less pain medication use, more mobility and increased function thus experiencing an easier rehabilitation. The researcher proposes another study including a larger sample size, double blinding, a second control group and testing using different population samples. This preliminary study does however reinforce a fascinating link between the mind and body.

Thornberry[65] conducted a chart review of 300 pain patients that had undergone hypnosis to help with symptoms. Seventy-nine men and 221 women's charts were examined to determine results of hypnotic intervention. Patients seen were from a largely rural, Appalachian and under-educated background. Charts were examined for their initial session of hypnotherapy only. Pain levels before treatment averaged 6.9, whereas post-hypnosis levels averaged 4.4. This is roughly a 36% reduction in pain levels. Patients also reported an average of 49.8% improvement in relaxation levels post-hypnosis. The researcher notes on the positive side that hypnosis is inexpensive with no side effects and gives control to the patient since hypnosis can be continued at home. It offers a way to empower patients to take control of their own pain management. Another key finding of the study was that patients from rural and less privileged backgrounds could learn the techniques and benefit from them. It was often suspected that only higher educated people could be hypnotized.

---

[65] Thornberry, T., Schaeffer, J., Wright, P., Haley, M., Kirsh, K. (2007). An exploration of the utility of hypnosis in pain management among rural pain patients. *Palliative and Supportive Care*, 5, 147-152.

Meditation and Mindfulness

We talked earlier in the book about doing mini meditations for health, but there is so much more that can be done in the field of meditation. Just the concept of mindfulness is something that we can incorporate into our lives and our practice. Are you truly present in each moment or are you mentally pushing the clock and thinking about the date you have that night? I know that it's hard to not let your mind wander to the future or past, but the more present you can be with what you are doing, the better your life will be.

Have you ever gotten to the end of your day and wondered if you've done something that you do every day like brush your teeth? It's something that we do so unconsciously that it sometimes doesn't even register that we have done it. Have you ever arrived at your destination and suddenly realized you have no recollection of driving there? Such things become so routine that they don't appear in our consciousness. Living life this way is a less than optimal state. It pulls us out of the present moment.

On the other hand, have you ever eaten an entire meal in a present mindful way? Feeling every morsel of food in your mouth, enjoying the textures, scents, and subtle flavors? Try it on a smaller scale. Take a dried cranberry, grape or cherry and really look at it. Notice the color, the visual texture of it. Then smell it, does it have any odor at all? Then put it in your mouth. Don't bite it yet. Just roll it around in your mouth and see how it feels. Smooth or rough? Is it perfectly round or some other shape? Now slowly bite into it. Does any juice emerge? Is it sweet, bitter, sour? Really taste it. That is being mindful.

If we can use mindfulness as an exercise, we can enhance our experiences and train our senses to be more heightened.

The concept of mindfulness meditation is a practice that allows you to be fully in the present moment without being hindered with thoughts of the past or the future. Often where our stress lies. Though mindful meditation is just one meditation technique, I was reminded recently at a meditation class, that it's not so much what happens on the pillow (during meditation), as how you live your life. I had the pleasure of studying for a weekend with Dr. Daniel Brown who has been studying and practicing meditation for almost four decades. Having never formally studied meditation, this was an eye-opening experience for me. Unlike minis, which I spoke of earlier, Dr. Brown taught a comprehensive meditation technique with specific hand positions, sitting still and concentrating on the breath. I was nervous going in. At first I was distracted and antsy and every sound in the room echoed through my head and that's all I could focus on. By the end of the second day, I had a glimpse of enlightenment.

During one of the question sessions someone asked how we could bring this to our clients and patients. And he answered that meditation isn't a commodity to sell to our clients, but a lineage technique that moves from master to student. He cautioned us against taking small bits of learning and trying to educate others with it. He believes that a student must have a master to track his progress and correct and encourage. This resonated greatly with me and after experiencing his teaching, I completely agree. Thus, if you want to pursue meditation to enhance your life or to teach others, I suggest you find an experienced practitioner and make meditation a part of your existence. More information about Dr. Daniel Brown can be found at www.danielbrownphd.com and information about his programs available www.pointingoutway.org.

More phenomenal information about mindful is also in John Kabat-Zinn's books, *Mindfulness for Beginners* and *Coming to Our Senses; Healing Ourselves and the World through Mindfulness*. And TM or Transcendental Meditation is one of the most common and popular forms of meditation. More information can be found at www.TM.org.

Since meditation is one of the most common relaxation techniques, here are some studies on the effects of meditation.

Orme-Johnson[66] studied meditation's effect on pain and imaged the brain to see what change it might induce. Long-term practitioners of Transcendental Meditation (TM) showed 40-50% less voxels (segments of the brain) responding to pain in the thalamus and total brain than in non-practitioners. After the controls learned TM their response decreased 40-50% in the thalamus, prefrontal cortex, total brain and marginally in the anterior cingulated cortex. All tests were done after, rather than during the session of meditation, thus eliminating the possibility of the cause being distraction. All participants stated the same level of pain, therefore indicating that meditation did not necessarily decrease the sensation of pain, but calmed the body's reaction to it. This study indicates that meditation might not cause the sensation of pain to be less, but that the body's reaction to it is better handled.

In a study by Morone[67] the effects of mindfulness meditation were tested on back pain sufferers. The intervention group received eight weekly mindfulness meditation sessions and homework assignments. The control group did not receive any intervention. Pain acceptance as measured by the Chronic Pain Acceptance Questionnaire improved significantly for the meditation group, while the control group worsened. The meditation group also showed significant improvement in physical function. The majority of participants opted to continue for another three months on

---

[66] Orme-Johnson, D., Schneider, R, Son, Y., Nidich, S., Cho, Z. (2006). Neuroimaging of meditation's effect on brain reactivity to pain. *Neuroreport, 17*(12), 1359-1363.

[67] Morone, N., Greco, C., Weiner, D. (2008). Mindfulness meditation for the treatment of chronic low back pain in older adults: A randomized controlled pilot study. *Pain, 134*(3), 310-319.

their own, obviously indicating not only enjoyment, but also benefits. This study proved that mind/body therapies such as meditation are a promising non-pharmaceutical option for pain treatment for older adults, but admittedly larger studies should be conducted.

Kabat-Zinn[68] provided an overview and background of what effects mindfulness meditation can have on various illnesses in the body. He sited one of his older studies where psoriasis sufferers listened to a meditation tape during their UV treatments[69]. They were asked to visualize the light slowing down and then stopping the rapidly growing skin cells. The control group received light treatments as usual with no suggestions. The meditators' skin cleared at approximately four times the rate of the non-meditators during the twelve-week study. A few of his conclusions are (1) Some factor or factors having to do with the mind can positively influence health. (2) Psychological participation on the part of the patient can lead to reduced healing in some patients. (3) The need for fewer light treatments reduces the risk of basal cell carcinoma, which is a risk of such treatments. (4) Since social support is minimal in this study, it cannot be considered a major factor in the observed outcome. He definitely recommends further study.

A study conducted by Ginandes[70] sought to discover if hypnosis could accelerate post-surgical wound healing. Eighteen otherwise healthy women about to undergo

---

[68] Kabat-Zinn, J. (2003). Mindfulness-based stress reduction (MBSR). *Constructivism in the Human Sciences, 8*(2), 73-107.

[69] Kabat-Zinn, J., Wheeler, E., Light, T., Skillings, A., et al. (1998). Influence of a mindfulness-based stress reduction intervention on rates of skin clearing in patients with moderate to severe psoriasis undergoing photo-therapy (UVB) and photochemotherapy (PUVA). *Psychosomatic Medicine*, 60, 625-632. (As cited by Kabat-Zinn, 2003).

[70] Ginandes, C., Brooks, P., Sando, W., Jones, C., Aker, J. (2003). Can medical hypnosis accelerate post-surgical wound healing? Results of a clinical trial. *American Journal of Clinical Hypnosis, 45*(4), 333-351.

reduction mammaplasty (breast reduction) were equally divided into three groups. The hypnosis group received eight half-hour weekly sessions commencing two weeks prior to surgery and continuing through six postoperative weeks. A hypnosis tape was provided to those participants and they were encouraged to use them daily. Suggestions for a smooth surgery, quick healing, diminished bleeding at the surgery site, etc. were reinforced during the pre-op sessions. Pain sensations were reframed as "sensations of healing." In the post-op sessions, healing was further encouraged with messages about tissue formation, collagen remodeling, wound contraction, etc. The psychological suggestions targeted "continued comfort, a return of energy and a sense of well-being."[71]

The second group received supportive attention for the same length of time as the first group but no hypnosis or home study tapes. The third group received no special intervention. Photos were taken of the individuals and there was also self-reported progress of healing. The three groups demonstrated significantly different rates of healing, with the hypnosis group far surpassing the others. The supportive attention group was second with the no intervention group showing the smallest amount of healing. In the subjective assessment of healing, those in the hypnosis group reported themselves as the fastest in wound healing and they experienced a quicker decrease in pain. The limitations of this study were the small study group and the absence of research into the cost effectiveness of adding hypnosis to treatment. Even with those limitations, they note a fascinating link between mind and body in augmenting healing.

---

[71] Ginandes, C., Brooks, P., Sando, W., Jones, C., Aker, J. (2003). Can medical hypnosis accelerate post-surgical wound healing? Results of a clinical trial. *American Journal of Clinical Hypnosis, 45*(4), 333-351.

Power of Prayer

I wanted to address the issue of prayer here because I know it is a big part of many people's lives. I don't pray, per se. I send out energy, I visualize, I do affirmations, I fantasize and I thank. Oh, I guess that is pretty much prayer.

There have been a few times that I have formally prayed with clients. Usually, it's a pretty serious situation where I detect a lot of fear and know that praying may help give them strength and balance. I have prayed mostly with my cancer clients where I feel that grounding them in their God will empower them to heal or to let go.

Though most people who pray claim to not be Christian, prayer usually has a strong religious connotation. Because prayer is such an individual thing and highly emotionally charged, I will just note some information that I found and leave this very personal matter to each individual and their God.

There are many that believe prayer can assist in healing others, even if they don't know they are being prayed for. As I mentioned earlier, doctors are know turning to the power of prayer for healing and encouraging their patients to pray. Dr. Herbert Benson, in *Timeless Healing; The Power of Biology and Belief* questions whether we are wired for God and prayer. He quotes a 1995 study from Dartmouth that stated that heart patients over fifty-five who were undergoing open-heart surgery had 3 times more to survive if they received solace and comfort from their religious beliefs.[72]

Multitudes of people believe in the power of prayer the same way others do the power of our thoughts. And the two are intermingled. Prayer is just another form of affirmations and positive thought. Seventy-six percent of people claim to pray on the regular basis according to a 1990

---

[72] Benson, H. *Timeless Healing*. Fireside Books. 1997. Pg. 173.

Gallup Pole. And it's true that religious people have reduced depression, alcohol use, drug use, hostility, anxiety, lower blood pressure, improved quality of life following a cancer or heart disease diagnosis, increased survival and improved coping skills. We also have to take into account the individual; you can be religious and still have negative, unhealthy thoughts and lead with your wounds. For more statistics, the following is an excerpt from Christian Healing Ministries website.[73] Although I was not able to substantiate all of these claims, I still felt it was good information on the subject.

• *More than 250 studies show that religious people are generally healthier than those who are not religious.*
• *130 studies support the fact that prayer is effective – it works!*
• *Distant prayer works as well as prayer in the recipient's presence.*
• *When you pray at a distance, the recipient doesn't even have to know that you are praying for it to be effective. However, if you enlist the faith of the person being prayed for, it does increase the prayer's effectiveness.*
• *A significant factor in healing is the love and compassion of the person praying. Love is meant to grow throughout our lives, so ministers of prayer who have more experience (of prayer and life) should, in general, prove to be more compassionate and more effective in prayer.*
• *Research shows that faith, a belief in what we are doing (or rather, what God is doing) does greatly affect the results. If you don't believe, nothing much is going to happen.*
• *Nevertheless, everyone can and should pray, and if the prayer is heart-felt, a first-time prayer can result in an astonishing healing.*
• *If you pray and meditate quietly every day for a period of time (such as twice a day for 15 minutes), you will increase*

---

[73]http://www.christianhealingmin.org/newsletter/archives/physical_healing/effectiveness.php

your own health, because prayer causes the "Relaxation Response" (popularized by Dr. Herbert Benson of Harvard), which results in lower blood pressure, fewer strokes, and fewer heart attacks.

The Christian Healing Ministries even state that if one doesn't pray for a sick person it should be considered medically unethical. While all of this might be too much for some people (especially non-Christians) to follow it has some valid points. First, let's say that the word prayer is interchangeable with words such as meditation, visualization and self-talk. That the more you practice these techniques, the better you get. Some people are innately better at it than others. This holds true for any of the mind/body techniques. And again, there are no side effects, it feels good and it can help others. The challenge of this particular aspect of mind/body medicine is that different religions often state that their approach is the only way. If all people, no matter what age, race, denomination or affiliation could recognize that in reality, all prayer/positive self-talk/visualization is good and find their own inner strength for healing that could be the future of prayer.

On the other hand, I found some recent studies that show prayer doesn't do a thing to help anyone. A 2006 New York Times article stated that a long awaited study on the effect of prayer on people undergoing heart surgery was ineffective.[74] In fact, when they were told they were being prayed for, it had deleterious effects. Spiritual people tend to make better lifestyle choices and live a bit longer. That might be attributed to the sense of community that exists within a church. Sense of community and social interaction has been proven to extend life. For now, it looks like the jury is still out whether the issue is faith and not prayer, whether prayer helps and whether people should be told that they are being prayed for. Bottom line is we naturally pray and send good

---

[74] http://www.nytimes.com/2006/03/31/health/31pray.html?
_r=pagewanted=print

thoughts to people in need. I think it's part of human nature and if we can affect water droplets and the AIDS virus with our mind, why shouldn't we be praying for each other and ourselves?

But Wait, There's More.

Now that we have covered some of the more popular mind/body therapies in detail, I want to discuss some additional techniques that you can investigate to enhance your mind/body health. If any of these pique your interest, it can certainly be worth connecting with a practitioner or at least doing more research. Remember to find someone with proper training in these techniques and not every one of these may resonate with you. Some may turn you off completely. I'm not advocating one over the other, just introducing options. Explore what feels comfortable to you!

Massage

Since my career started in massage, I wanted to talk about how it can enhance your health and help your relax. Right off the bat, it is a physical modality that is known to relax muscles and decrease tension. It also lengthens muscles, moves blood and lymph, releases toxins, and helps release feel good hormones in the brain. Massage can either be used for purely physical purposes or include the mind, it's completely up to you. Be clear with your massage therapist if you want a certain type of meditative music, a certain scent of aromatherapy or an eye pillow. You can decide if you want to talk or be quiet and go inside. Perhaps there is a meditation tape that you'd like to listen to you or your massage therapist can walk you through a visualization during your treatment. Regardless of what you choose, remember that it's your time and you must communicate your needs and preferences. Be specific and clear. And if you don't like one practitioner, move on to find another more suited to you. It's your time and money and you deserve the best. Since there are so many massage options, here are some of the most common.

Swedish is the most basic massage technique. It addresses the outer layer of muscle, therefore doesn't go as deep or effect as much change on the body as other techniques. Also considered classic massage, this is what you are going to get in most spas. It tends to be the least expensive on the menu and also in my opinion the least effective for physical change, however it is great for overall relaxation, a feel good massage.

Deep tissue tends to be an upcharge in spas and it addresses the deeper layers of muscle. Contrary to popular belief it doesn't have to hurt. Deep tissue is not just harder Swedish and takes extra training. If you want this modality make sure the practitioner knows what he/she is doing. You can get hurt with an inexperienced therapist. Good for injuries and rehab if the therapist is well trained.

Hot stone is a popular spa treatment. Though few massage therapists do it, it accounts for the most injuries and massage law suits. I'm not a fan of this modality as you can get burned or an inexperienced therapist can't feel the tissue beneath the stone and goes too deep. Personally, I find this pointless. (Just my opinion) There are many that say the heat from the stones relax you more, but I'm just not sure it does much.

Shiatsu is Japanese massage, which is done fully clothed on mats on the floor. It involves acupressure points, compression and is great for balancing the body. It is more used for balancing chi and less for physical ailments. Not done much anymore that I've seen and some spas have adapted it for a table, which confuses people because then they go to an actual shiatsu practitioner and are stunned they are dressed on the floor.

No matter which massage technique you choose, remember to communicate your needs and use it as your time connect body and mind.

Biofeedback

Although I have never formally practiced biofeedback, I believe the modality is worth considering.

The following Material on Biofeedback was provided through: U.S. Department of Health and Human Services Division of Communications and Education, National Institute of Mental Health Public Health Service - Alcohol, Drug Abuse and Mental Health, Administration 5600 Fishers Lane, Rockville, MD 20857 USA, DHHS Publication No (ADM) 83-1273. This Material was written by Bette Runck, staff writer, Division of Communication and Education, National Institute of Mental Health. NATIONAL INSTITUTE OF MENTAL HEALTH- Division of Scientific and Public Information-Plain Talk Series- Ruth Kay

Please contact the organizations listed at the end of this section about how you can use biofeedback.

Biofeedback is a treatment technique in which people are trained to improve their health by using signals from their own bodies. Physical therapists use biofeedback to help stroke victims regain movement in paralyzed muscles. Psychologists use it to help tense and anxious clients learn to relax. Specialists in many different fields use biofeedback to help their patients cope with pain.

Chances are you have used biofeedback yourself. You've used it if you have ever taken your temperature or stepped on a scale. The thermometer tells you whether you're running a fever, the scale whether you've gained weight. Both devices "feed back" information about your body's condition. Armed with this information, you can take steps you've learned to improve the condition. When you're running a fever, you go to bed and drink plenty of fluids.

When you've gained weight, you resolve to eat less and sometimes you do.

Clinicians rely on complicated biofeedback machines in somewhat the same way that you rely on your scale or thermometer. Their machines can detect a person's internal bodily functions with far greater sensitivity and precision than a person can alone. This information may be valuable. Both patients and therapists use it to gauge and direct the progress of treatment.

For patients, the biofeedback machine acts as a kind of sixth sense that allows them to "see" or "hear" activity inside their bodies. One commonly used type of machine, for example, picks up electrical signals in the muscles. It translates these signals into a form that patients can detect: It triggers a flashing light bulb, perhaps, or activates a beeper every time muscles grow tenser. If patients want to relax tense muscles, they try to slow down the flashing or beeping.

Like a pitcher learning to throw a ball across a home plate, the biofeedback trainee, in an attempt to improve a skill, monitors the performance. When a pitch is off the mark, the ballplayer adjusts the delivery so that he performs better the next time he tries. When the light flashes or the beeper beeps too often, the biofeedback trainee makes internal adjustments, which alter the signals. The biofeedback therapist acts as a coach, standing at the sidelines setting goals and limits on what to expect and giving hints on how to improve performance.

Scientists cannot yet explain how biofeedback works. Most patients who benefit from biofeedback are trained to relax and modify their behavior. Most scientists believe that relaxation is a key component in biofeedback treatment of many disorders, particularly those brought on or made worse by stress. Their reasoning is based on what is known about the effects of stress on the body. In brief, the argument goes like this: Stressful events produce strong emotions, which arouse certain physical responses. Many of these responses are controlled by the sympathetic nervous system, the network of nerve tissues that helps prepare the body to meet emergencies by "flight or fight."

The typical pattern of response to emergencies probably emerged during the time when all humans faced mostly physical threats. Although the "threats" we now live with are seldom physical, the body reacts as if they were: The pupils dilate to let in more light. Sweat pours out, reducing the chance of skin cuts. Blood vessels near the skin contract to reduce bleeding, while those in the brain and muscles dilate to increase the oxygen supply. The gastrointestinal tract, including the stomach and intestines, slows down to reduce the energy expensed in digestion. The heart beats faster, and blood pressure rises. Normally, people calm down when a stressful event is over, especially if they have done something to cope with it. For instance, imagine your own reactions if you're walking down a dark street and hear someone running toward you. You get scared. Your body prepares you to ward off an attacker or run fast enough to get away. When you do escape, you gradually relax.

If you get angry with your boss, it's a different matter. Your body may prepare to fight. But since you want to keep your job, you try to ignore the angry feelings. Similarly, if on the way home you get stalled in traffic, there's nothing you can do to get away. These situations can literally make you sick. Your body has prepared for action, but cannot act. Individuals differ in the way they respond to stress. In some, one function, such as blood pressure, becomes more active while others remain normal. Many experts believe that these individual physical responses to stress can become habitual. When the body is repeatedly aroused, one or more functions may become permanently overactive. Actual damage to bodily tissues may eventually result.

Biofeedback is often aimed at changing habitual reactions to stress that can cause pain or disease. Many clinicians believe that some of their patients and clients have forgotten how to relax. Feedback of physical responses such *as skin temperature and muscle tension provides information to help patients recognize a relaxed state. The feedback signal may also act as a kind of reward for reducing tension. It's like a piano teacher whose frown turns to a smile when a young musician finally plays a tune properly.*

The value of a feedback signal as information and reward may be even greater in the treatment of patients with paralyzed or spastic muscles. With these patients, biofeedback seems to be primarily a form of skill training like learning to pitch a ball. Instead of watching the ball, the patient watches the machine, which monitors activity in the affected muscle. Stroke victims with paralyzed arms and legs, for example, see that some part of their affected limbs remains active. The signal from the biofeedback machine proves it. This signal can guide the exercises that help patients regain use of their limbs. Perhaps just as important, the feedback convinces patients that the limbs are still alive. This reassurance often encourages them to continue their efforts. <End excerpt>

More information about Biofeedback can be found at the following organizations:

The Association for Applied Psychophysiology and Biofeedback (formerly the Biofeedback Society of America)
10200 W. 44th Avenue
Suite 304
Wheat Ridge, CO 80033-2840
Phone: 1-800-477-8892 / 303-422-8436
Fax: 303-422-8894
E-mail: AAPB@resourcenter.com
Internet: http://www.aapb.org

AAPB is the national membership association for professionals using biofeedback. AAPB holds a national meeting, offers CE programs, produces a journal and newsmagazine and other biofeedback related publications.

The Biofeedback Certification Institute of America
10200 W. 44th Avenue
Suite 304
Wheat Ridge, CO 80033-2840

The BCIA was established as an independent agency to provide national certification for biofeedback providers.

Earlier on page 52 I discussed Bio Dots. Interestingly BioDots are basically mini biofeedback devices. As mentioned they are a very useful tool for gauging our emotions and stress levels.

There are a lot of people now doing neurobiofeedback, where you can actually retrain the brain. It's good for anxiety, addiction and PTSD.

Progressive Muscle Relaxation

This is an incredibly simple but useful technique for calming the mind and the body. This involves starting with a part of the body, typically the feet and tightening them for a count of five and then releasing, moving up to the calves and tightening for a count of five and then releasing. You move progressively up the body, taking body part by body part and tensing and relaxing them. This helps you pay attention to the stress in those parts of the body and helping to dissipate it. This technique that was founded in the 1920s has been useful for such things as irritable bowel syndrome, headaches and general tension. This is also a great way to relax to fall asleep. There is so much great information on line about this easy and useful method of relaxation, here is a great site: http://www.guidetopsychology.com/pmr.htm.

Chakra Healing

The chakras (meaning wheel in Sanskrit) are energy centers that occupy seven places on the body, starting at the base of the spine and moving up to the top of the head. Most practitioners acknowledge that there are many more than seven, but those are the ones that are usually addressed with healing. The chakras spin clockwise when they are healthy and balanced. These energy centers also correspond to colors, organs, thought processes and sounds. When I do reiki, I concentrate on rebalancing the chakras and check them using a pendulum, which tells me if the chakras are spinning the right direction. Theoretically, you can tell if someone's body or mind is out of sorts, simply by checking the chakras. For example, we spoke earlier about word use/disease correspondences. If someone isn't speaking their truth, or feels like they have a lump in their throat, they may develop a thyroid issue. I wouldn't be surprised to find the throat chakra to be closed off at that point. Opening the chakra can allow for healing to occur in that area of the body and you may find that you are more easily able to speak, sing, swallow and breath. Many energy practitioners work with the chakras and there is a technique called chakra clearing that can be incorporated. Though I can't say there is any strong science behind working with the chakras, I have seen evidence that changes in the energy does seem to affect the physical body and the thought processes. For your information, here are the chakras and their correspondences:

Root Chakra: Base of the spine, red, corresponds to finances, career, issues of physical security, physical safety and having your needs met. It's basic survival issues.

Sacral Chakra: Midway between the naval and the base of the spine, orange, sex, physical pleasure, empathizing with others emotions, thoughts about your appearance.

Solar Plexus Chakra: Found right behind the naval, yellow, power, control, relates to the adrenal glands, fear surrounding control and others controlling you.

Heart Chakra: It is the first of the upper chakras that correspond to spiritual issues as opposed to physical ones. Green, relationships, love, physical attachment, forgiveness, co-dependency or obsession. I commonly find that people who just experienced a loss or breakup have a heart chakra that is closed or spinning the wrong direction.

Throat Chakra: Adam's apple area, blue, speaking your truth, communication of all kinds, artistic work, connected with the thyroid, saying what you feel, self-expression.

Brow Chakra: Is located at your third eye and is connected with the pituitary. This is the chakra of consciousness, indigo and where you would see ashes on Ash Wednesday or a bindi in the Middle Eastern faiths. This is where you are looking during a formal meditation. Through this chakra individual consciousness is expanded into universal consciousness.

Crown Chakra: Top of the head, Vivid purple, this is how we receive thoughts from the divine or collective consciousness; it's the wealth of creativity. This chakra is affected by thoughts relating to God, religion, spirituality, trust and divine guidance.

You'll notice that the chakras correspond to the colors of the rainbow; red, orange, yellow, green, blue, indigo, violet. You remember ROYGBIV don't you?

There are books of meditations you can do to clear and balance your own chakras or seek out a practitioner that can help.

Color Healing

We all have favorite colors or different emotional reactions to color. Restaurants, hospitals, offices, advertisers are all very aware of how color effects our mood. Bright colors like yellow and red invigorate us and make us feel happy. Dark colors like browns and greens are more grounding and earthy. We can use color for healing, either by having it in our environment as a wall color, or using the colors that correspond to the chakras that we just spoke of. Using them as gemstones and crystals or even drinking color-charged water is another option. Color is something that could easily be incorporated into your life if you feel drawn to it. Here are some basic color correspondences:

Red: warming, invigorating
Orange: not as harsh as red, but contains many of its properties
Yellow: a mild sedative, gives a mental uplift
Green: healing color, general tonic and invigorator
Blue: antiseptic, cooling, good for inflammation,
Indigo: removes fears of the mind and great for people afraid of the dark, great for emotions
Violet: good for the nervous system

Again, you can surround yourself with these colors or use a gemstone of the corresponding color. There are so many great resources on line for finding more color correspondences. Here is one I found particularly interesting http://www.crystalinks.com/colors.html.

Reiki, an Ancient Tradition

Reiki is a hands-on healing energy technique where universal energy or chi, comes through the practitioner and into the person being healed. It heals on all levels of body, mind and spirit. It is relaxing, balancing and strengthening.

I had my first Reiki attunement in 1994 from a teacher in Los Angeles named Diane Vaughn (No one has been able to find her for years so if you are her, or know her, please contact me). An attunement is basically another name for the initiation/procedure to give the healer the ability to use Reiki. An attunement consists of symbols placed in the hands and head of the soon-to-be healer. The attunement itself is a quick process, which only takes a few minutes. However, most Reiki teachers spend several hours if not days with the practitioner before the actual attunement.

There are three levels of Reiki: I, II and III (master level). The first level gives you the ability to practice on yourself and others. The second provides you with symbols to enhance the practice and also work from a distance, and the third attunement teaches you how to teach others. That is called the master level and unlike the name implies, does not make someone at that level superior to others at the lower stages. It simply means that they can pass attunements and teach others.

Reiki, meaning Universal Light Energy, is thought to be as ancient as humankind itself and its roots are steeped in myth. It is based on a master/teacher relationship and on initiations of the students. Reiki was re-discovered by a man that was looking for answers. Mikao Usui, a Christian minister and university professor, wanted to know how Jesus did his healing. A ten-year quest abroad and a seven-year search in the United States proved useless; no information could be found. Usui decided to embark on a journey.

He returned to Japan where he studied ancient texts in a Zen Monastery but knew he needed to go through the "test." The test was a three week fast and meditation on a mountain. On the final morning of his quest, slightly before sunrise, Usui saw a bolt of light coming from the sky directly towards him. He felt fear and wanted to run but realized this is what he had been waiting for. The light struck his forehead over his third eye and Usui lost consciousness. He saw millions of colorful bubbles and the Reiki symbols appeared to him along with information about how to use them. It was the first Reiki attunement.

Usui took Reiki through the streets of Japan and spent the next several years traveling, healing, and sharing his story. It was believed that Usui made sixteen-eighteen Reiki masters in his career but only one, Chujiro Hayashi, was mentioned in most Reiki sources and was Usui's successor. This man went on to teach Reiki, open a healing clinic and made sixteen masters in his lifetime.

Though information on Reiki, once kept secret, is available in every bookstore and on countless websites, even EBay, it is a unique skill in that you must have someone teach you. You can read all the books you want, but without the hands-on attunement, it just won't work. I do believe that some people are born with Reiki ability, but I still think having a teacher, a guide, is necessary. It helps you to hone your skill and provides you with more focus and intention.

How Reiki works is pretty simple. You place your hands on the person (or above the body) with the intention of healing, and the energy starts to flow. It feels like a heat and tingling in the hands. There is usually a deep sense of relaxation for the person enjoying the session and they may even fall asleep. Sometimes laughter or tears comes too. Reiki can only be used for positive purposes and can't harm in any way. It enhances and accelerates the body's healing ability and balances the chi.

Most people who practice Reiki are in the healing arts, but many lay people learn it to help with family, friends or personal development. Reiki is great for children, plants and animals. It can help with emotional healing after a loss or breakup, physical healing to speed the process and on a spiritual level to provide grounding or focus. Reiki practitioners exist in practically every city in the world and are easy to locate on the Internet or in health-related publications.

If you are looking for a Reiki healing session, ask the practitioner how long they have been practicing and what level they have been taught. Some use crystals and other accouterments; ask what their healing involves in advance. Though it is not as important these days, people used to put great importance on tracing their lineage to one of the original teachers. You should know though what the healer's background is and where they studied. Make sure you feel a connection with them and trust them, or seek another healer.

If you want to learn Reiki, seek out a seasoned, level III master. Someone should not be teaching others without years of practice. Ask if your attunement involves a healing session first, which is how I practice and if handouts are included. Also, make sure they can give you a certificate, especially if you want to be a practitioner yourself. You may want to meet the person before committing to the attunement and if you don't feel a good connection, seek guidance elsewhere. There are now many versions of Reiki, slightly different symbols, different names, and different methods. A strict group believes Reiki should be exclusive and expensive. Others give hundreds of people attunements in a weekend at a campsite. For $75 you can become a Reiki Master on EBay. (Please don't do that.) Reiki is becoming more mainstream and even hospitals and cancer centers are now embracing Reiki's healing and research is being carried out on its success rates. The website for information about where you can find a Reiki practitioner and become involved is www.centerforreikiresearch.org.

If you are interested in other similar energy techniques, check out pranic healing and healing touch.

These are just a few of the many energy techniques you can utilize for healing.

Crystal Healing

Gemstones and crystals have long been thought to have healing, even magical properties. Some use stones for their color, others believe different types of stones have different uses and others still believe that each stone has a unique spirit. I use gemstones and crystals during my reiki treatments as my teacher did. Healing with crystals could fill many books, but here are some of the basics, as I understand them. Stones can be placed on the chakras as we discussed previously to help balance and heal them. Many people carry stones in small pouches or on necklaces to utilize their properties and others have jewelry made of the specific stones.

-Clear quartz is the most common and is used generally to energize, enhance, stabilize and calm the mind.
-Hematite, commonly made into rings, is thought to ground the person and energize the physical body.
-Ruby is thought to balance the heart and enhance circulation; it enhances confidence, security and self-esteem.
-Rose quartz, another incredibly common stone, is great for releasing emotional stress. It can help heal the body by removing stress that might be built up. I use this stone for clients that have suffered a loss, especially romantically.
-Citrine is one of my favorite stones. It's thought to balance, and be warm, soothing and integrating. It decreases irritation, creates optimism and relaxation through the body.
-Emerald is a great stone for meditation and brings calm by removing hidden fears.
-Turquoise is one of the most universal and oldest of gemstone amulets worn for protection.[75]

---

[75] Lilly, S and S. *Healing with Crystals and Chakra Energy*. Hermes House 2005.

-Amethyst is another favorite stone being calming and stabilizing for the mind. It can reduce restlessness, irritation and worry. It's useful for meditation and thought to dispel alcoholism.

It is believed you should cleanse your crystals occasionally as they are thought to attract the energies of the person using them. They can be cleansed in water, in moonlight, on another larger crystal or with salt. I make sure I wash my stones after I use them on a client just to insure that no energies are then transferred to the next client I use them for.

More information about crystals can be found on line and in numerous publications.

Bach Flower Essences

Bach Flower Essences are a little different than the other modalities we have been speaking of in that they are not a hands-on technique. I use them quite a bit in my practice and wanted to share information about them. I charge very little to put together a formula and I've seen them work wonders. There is also a method of Bach Flower massage, which I've never done, but heard is quite effective. Enjoy this information about this great treatment option.

In the 1930's Edward Bach, a medical doctor and bacteriologist, discovered Bach Flower Essences. He used thirty-eight individual flowers plus a combination of five flowers he called *Rescue Remedy*. Dr. Bach's healing theories were cutting edge for the time. He believed that people had the ability to heal themselves and that anyone could use the flower remedies. He chose plants with what he believed to be high vibration and expected them to heal through that vibration. He ignored physical symptoms, instead focusing on disharmonies of energy. To him, the principles of unity, perfection and harmony meant more than disease, dysfunction and sickness. Dr. Bach's healing strategy was "Don't fight it, transform it" and he achieved that through his simple remedies.

The essences work on the emotional state of the person, transforming the negative into positive. These negative states can lead to disease and though Bach Flower Essences don't address physical issues, they can stave off illness through balancing the spiritual/emotional state.

To use the remedies typically the client fills out a questionnaire and the chosen remedies are determined by those answers. I equate this process to the keys on a piano. We are all born with emotional "notes." Stressful events and people in our lives such as an alcoholic father, abusive stepparent, mental illness in the family and early losses are equivalent to pounding on certain keys of the emotional piano. With so much pounding the keys eventually get out of tune. Flower essences are used to retune our emotional piano.

The chosen essences are mixed into a master bottle and are taken four times a day. It is not recommended to use more than seven flowers in a combination at a time. Often the emotions unfold like an onion and as you balance some emotional states different ones will appear. It's good to reevaluate the formula after a few weeks and make any necessary changes. I've noticed that people will just suddenly stop taking the remedy or lose it. This seems to indicate that a new formula is needed.

There are numerous advantages to Bach Flower Essences:

-You get quick results. I've seen change in a matter of hours. Rescue Remedy works very quickly and has gotten me through two weddings, one divorce, numerous funerals, near car accidents, and a knife in my hand. It's good stuff!!!

-They are affordable. Each remedy costs about $14 and can be found at health food stores and on line. You can also purchase the full series of remedies to mix for yourself and others. That runs between $415 and $600 depending on whether you want the stylish leather case.

-If it doesn't work, there are no side effects. It simply won't do anything.

-The essences don't interact with other medications or therapies, though you should still tell your physician you are taking them. Be prepared to explain what they are.

-You can do it yourself, though the input and expertise of a trained professional is always recommended.

-They are great for kids and pets. I had a client that used Rescue Remedy for her nervous horse; she would just put it in his water. They now make alcohol free Rescue Remedy for pets and kids. If alcohol is a problem for you, place in warm water to evaporate it.

-This is customized medicine, not one-size-fits-all therapy. There are millions of combinations that can be made from those thirty-eight flowers. For example, there are at least five different remedies that can be chosen for depression depending on the cause and type.

When I recommend flower essences for clients I have them fill out the questionnaire. I review their answers, ask more questions and try to determine what the best combination will be for them. I mix the formula and give them a hand out that tells them what flowers are in the formula, what conditions they are being used for, directions on how to take it and I also include empowering statements or affirmations. I often recommend certain activities like gardening, deep breathing, walking or vigorous exercise depending on the symptoms and the formula. (See example form below.)

The consultation can be done over the phone, but in person is better to observe body language and physical reaction during the interview. I follow up with the client in a few days and we reevaluate in two weeks. Usually I change the formula at that time.

Excerpt from real protocol.

Centaury: Neglecting your own needs and difficulty saying no (what the flower is for.)
Anytime anyone asks for something ask, "What are his or her real motives? And what do I really want?" (The first phrase is a recommendation, these next are affirmations.)
"I am solely responsible for my own development"
"I stand up for my own needs"

Elm: Overwhelmed
Provide more breaks when planning your work
"I am up to the situation"
"I always have the help I need"

Oak: Sense of duty, neglect own needs
Do exercises for neck and shoulder area
"I shall do it"

"Energy is flowing to me from the primal source"

Dr. Bach's essences are not the only ones out there; there are other similar protocols to be found. Australian Bush Flowers are another popular group that uses between sixty-five and sixty-nine essences from Australian flowers. I found others that were invented and mixed by individuals. Practitioners can range from the self-taught to those "channeling the counsel of elders" to licensed and formally taught homeopaths and other natural health practitioners.

If you would like to learn more about this system, there are Bach Foundation approved courses that are taught in locations around the United States and also distance learning opportunities. There are practitioners in practically every city to help you with this process. There is also an endless supply of books written on the subject. I've listed a few of my favorites below.

The Bach Remedies Repertory by Wheeler
The Encyclopedia of Bach Flower Therapy by Scheffer (Very thorough!)
Heal Thyself by Bach
Bach Flower Remedies by Bach
The Bach Remedies Workbook By Ball
Bach Flower Massage by Lo Rito

For more information:

Bach Flower website, www.bachflower.com and www.bachcentre.com

Homeopathics

Homeopathy is one of my favorite systems of medicine. It can also be an intricate system of medicine. Therefore I recommend you finding a qualified homeopathic practitioner for your needs. Steve Brynoff, traditional naturopath, has had over 20 years experience with this form of natural healing. The following is in his words.

Seven out of ten people feel stressed or anxious daily. The terms 'stress' and 'anxiety' are often used interchangeably. While it can be difficult to differentiate between the two, they are not the same thing. Stress is the body's response to an event or a change. Hans Selye distinguished between positive stress (eustress) and negative stress (distress). According to the National Institutes of Health, stress results from a specific, clearly defined trigger event that results in a feeling of frustration, irritability, inability to focus, sweating, stomach upset and perhaps a headache or increased heart rate. These may be events such as riding a roller coaster, encountering the bully on the playground or being involved in a car accident. Usually the feelings of stress pass once the stressor is gone.

Anxiety is a general feeling of apprehension, fear or worry, often with a vague or undefined cause or trigger. Because of the lack of a trigger event, anxiety is referred to as a mental condition. There are many types of anxiety disorders, such as obsessive-compulsive disorder, panic disorder, generalized anxiety disorder and phobias. Physical symptoms of anxiety can include palpitations, faster heartbeat and muscle tension; mental symptoms may include fatigue, apprehension or an inability to concentrate. Unlike stress, the feeling of anxiety may persist with or without a stressor.

Stress can also be cumulative; stressors that don't go away can create anxiety. While there is overlap in the symptoms, the main differentiating factors include a precipitating cause (present for stress, absent for anxiety) and duration (stress goes away when the stressor leaves, anxiety may persist for a much longer time). *Emotional states are strongly impacted by homeopathic remedies, and in classical homeopathy, are the preeminent symptom to consider (according to Hahnemann, the founder of Homeopathy). The more closely the symptoms can match the remedy, the better the remedy will function. I generally recommend lower potencies because of the acute nature of stress.*

Aconitum Napellus
Emotional stress, fear, anxiety, anguish of the mind, frightful, excitable, claustrophobic, panic.

Argentum Nitricum
Anxiety from anticipation of a pending big event.

Arsenicum Album
Irritable weakness, exhaustion, fear, worry, guilt or resentment, transitional uncertainty, blaming, critical, restless, paranoid.

Aurum Metallicum
Failure, guilt, loneliness, loss, shame, depression, betrayal, ambitious, lacking self-confidence, suicidal.

Avena Sativa
Nervous debility and exhaustion.

Impatiens Glandulifera
Speed performance, nervous tension, nervous exhaustion.

Pulsatilla
General insecurities or clinginess, tearful, hormone-related stress

Kali Phosphoricum
Anxiety and nervous dread, headache, insomnia, feelings of

dread, fear of not being able to cope.

Gelsemium
Trembling, mental dullness, chills, perspiration, diarrhea, fear of crowds or falling.

Adrenalinum
Support adrenal function.

Apis Mellifica
Brain feels very tired. Great inclination to sleep but cannot.

Selenium Metallicum
Mental labor fatigues. Headache. Liver disorders. Skin disorders.

Phosphorous
Overwork, changes of mood, hot flushes or palpitations, loneliness, nervousness around others, overextended to the point of exhaustion.

*Please remember to consult your physician or therapist if you are feeling severe depression, distress or are having suicidal thoughts.

Aromatherapy

Incorporating scent into world is incredibly common. I'm not talking about spraying fake air freshener, but taking advantage of the amazing natural scents that this world provides. You can use diffusers, pillows, sachets, baths and just straight oils. And it's not just to smell good or cover up a stale house; scents can be used for healing. This field is so vast; I talked with Jane Hendler of AJNE in Carmel, CA, an organic perfumer and master essential oil therapist. The following is in her fabulous words.

Scent has been a vital piece of my being as long as I can remember...Growing up in the Midwest I recollect picnics while sitting under the wafting magnolia tree and the scent of roses at my grandparents garden, playing with my dolls on a blanket in front of our amazing hedge of lilac bushes and the smell of fresh cut grass on Saturday summer mornings. I love how scent brings me back to a moment in time and to the people that I have loved so dearly. A mere whiff of one of these scents touches my heart and brings tears of delight to my eyes. My entire life is built around scent memories. I suspect that we all have a dominant sense and this is most definitely mine.

The sense of smell takes one into the ancient reptilian part of the brain called the limbic system or more commonly referred to as the right brain. This is the part of the brain that connects to memory and emotion. Studies have shown that this part of the brain is apparently 10 times more powerful than our other senses when it comes to memory and emotion. It's totally non linear and is also rather spacey and doesn't at all equate to time. It's a glorious part of the brain that is like a beautiful fairy tale in an olfactory kind of way whisking us away to heart felt memories. In fact, I caution my clients after one of our blending sessions to sit for a while before embarking on other projects as the brain will need to reluctantly return to the left side in order to function completely in our busy world.

I started on my journey to understand and study essential oil therapy also referred to as aromatherapy about 20 years ago. Since this time I have completed classes and degrees from many of these masters, my favorite being The College of Botanical Healing Arts in Santa Cruz created and led by Elizabeth Jones.

My husband Rex Rombach has been on this path with me since the very beginning and joined me in this passion and/or obsession 10 years ago when we decided to create our current business Ajne Parfumerie and Apothecary based in Carmel California. It was a perfect match combined with my passion and expertise in blending the essential oils in a system to match a client's emotional and/or physical needs either in a perfumic, therapeutic or industrial diffused blend and Rex's passion to grow and distill plants, develop the body care formulas and create the marketing. Since the inception of Ajne we have been creating ready-to-wear and custom blended organic parfum, body care, skincare and environmental fragrance both for individuals and corporations.

It's quite amazing how the world is now embracing natural, organic and local creations vs. the industrialized synthetic products of the past. It's funny that people are just finally beginning to understand that our skin is our biggest organ and everything that we apply to it goes into our bloodstream almost immediately. Not to mention that our nose is the most direct connection to our brain so whatever we smell affects every neurotransmitter and receptor in our entire body. Studies have shown that at least 17% of the public has allergic reactions to synthetic scents. Most people don't really know why, but the simple truth is that synthetic scent is made up of petroleum particles and plasticizers. Bottom line, there is a body burden after cumulative exposure to toxic chemicals and materials like these.

Let's get to basics with understanding nature and essential oils. The first questions that most people ask me *are...what are essential oils, how can they be used and what is important to know about them? Here are the very basics so you can begin converting your life from aromachemicals to natural pure essential oils... An essential oil is a concentrated liquid containing volatile aromatic compounds extracted from plants. It is basically the true essence or scent of the plant. Essential oils are antifungal, antiviral and antiseptic. They protect the plant from predators by repelling with scent and they aid in reproduction by attracting with their scent. They also serve as the immune system to the plant and offer natural hydration. They are powerful substances that can positively affect all body systems via the brain through inhalation or via the blood stream by application to the skin. Essential oils may be produced by distillation, expression, CO_2 or solvent extraction. Essential oils are used in perfumery, aromatherapy, cosmetics, incense, for flavoring food and beverages, natural medicine and household cleaning products. They were some of the original medicines prior to pharmaceutical drugs and the original materials used in the making of perfumes and fragrances prior to chemical renditions.*

HOW TO USE ESSENTIAL OILS

Environment/Ambient Scent
- ~ *Use undiluted in an electric diffuser to scent up to a 1000 square foot space*
- ~ *Use undiluted in a tea candle diffuser to scent a 100 square foot space*
- ~ *Use undiluted in a light bulb ring to scent a 10 square foot space*
- ~ *Use undiluted in small pottery pieces to diffuse small spaces and drawers*
- ~ *Use undiluted in a lighter plug in a car diffuser*
- ~ *Add several drops to natural potpourri and sachets to scent small spaces, drawers and laundry driers*
- ~ *Add several drops to bedding, carpets, bath towels, etc. (be aware of staining on light colored fabrics)*

~ *Add several drops to the wet wax of an unscented candle after extinguishing; allow wax to harden before relighting*

~ *Add several drops in toilet bowl*

~ *Fill sink with hot water and add several drops of essential oil to refresh bathroom or kitchen*

~ *Mix 5-10% (37-75 drops per ounce) in a sprayer with (equal parts) 5-10% unscented body wash and distilled water for a natural room freshener*

Personal Fragrances

~ *Add 10-30% (75-225 drops to 1 ounce) in jojoba oil or various oils to create your own natural perfume*

Bodycare/Skincare/Haircare
(Use for fragrance and/or therapeutic health issues)

~ *Add up to 2% (15 drops per 1 ounce) in unscented lotion, shower gel, bath salts, powders, bath oil, body oil, scalp oil, shampoo and conditioner*

~ *Use 1-2 drops neat (undiluted) Lavender, Rosewood, Peppermint or Teatree for skincare and/or therapeutic treatment*

~ *Add 10 drops or more to bath or hot tub*

~ *Add .5% (4 drops per 1ounce) to skincare to treat various skin conditions*

Contraindications

~ *Avoid all essential oils during first trimester of pregnancy*

~ *Avoid the following oils throughout pregnancy: Aniseed, Basil, Birch, Cedarwood, Clary sage, Cypress, Fennel, Hyssop, Jasmine, Juniper, Marjoram, Myrrh, Peppermint, Parsley, Rosemary, Sage, Tarragon and Thyme*

~ *Be aware to use lower percentages such as .5% (4 drops per 1 ounce) or less on small children and pets.*

~ *Be aware not to apply oils directly on the skin neat except for the essential oil of Lavender, Rosewood, Peppermint and Teatree.*

Essential Oil Blends for Therapeutic Purposes (Jane's Favorites!)

Muscle Joint Relief/Arthritis: Lavender, Birch, Peppermint, Rosemary

Energize: Rosemary, Peppermint, Ginger, Basil

Meditation: Myrrh, Frankincense, Sandalwood, Cedarwood

Digestion: Peppermint, Ginger, Fennel

Immune Boost: Ginger, Cinnamon, Bay Laurel and Thyme

Sleep Ease: Chamomile, Lavender, Marjoram, Valerian

Menopause: Geranium, Fennel, Sage, Basil

PMS: Clary Sage, Lavender, Marjoram, Geranium

Baby Blend: Lavender and Rosewood

For more information visit www.ajne.com.

T'ai Chi Chuan

If you drive by many parks on a Sunday afternoon you may see large groups of people moving their arms in harmony. They are practicing the beautiful art form of Tai Chi. This slow moving, relaxing martial art is sometimes called "meditation in motion" because it promotes serenity during its practice of gentle movements. Tai Chi has many different styles and is a series of postures and movements that flow effortlessly one into the other. Though we think of Tai Chi as unhurried and gentle, it is a martial art like Karate or Ju Jitsu and was originally practiced for defense. There are systems that are faster and can also incorporate weapons like a staff or sword.

Tai Chi is considered safe and gentle, which is why many elderly practice it and it is available for study at many adult education courses and YMCAs around the country. Three of the key elements of Tai Chi are body posture and gentle movement, breath regulation and meditation or purposeful relaxation. Multiple studies have shown that just some of the benefits are:

-Reducing anxiety, depression and stress
-Improving balance, flexibility and muscle strength
-Reducing falls in older people
-Improving sleep
-Lowering blood pressure
-Improving cardiac fitness in older adults
-Relieving chronic pain
-Increasing endurance, energy and agility
-Improving overall feelings of well-being

And there is no special equipment to buy or large expenses. You can do Tai Chi anywhere once you learn the art and clearly it has numerous benefits. In fact, doesn't it sound like the Relaxation Response that we've been talking about? You bet! And Tai Chi was one of the modalities I studied at Harvard with Peter Wayne, PhD.

My client Sylvia Perlee had this to say about her experience with Tai Chi, "Tai Chi feels wonderful; it calms my mind and helps me let go of tension. I feel centered and connected with the earth. Tai Chi lifts my spirit."

Yoga

Yoga has become a very mainstream modality that you can find in almost every town in this country whether at your gym, adult education center or the local YMCA. There are so many traditions and styles of Yoga I can't even begin to cover them here. Let's just say that Yoga is a great system to balance body and mind (and bring in the breath) and is a great healing modality for many. I recommend a trained instructor who can give individual attention and has full knowledge of any physical restrictions or injuries that the client has.

Since I am just a fan and not a Yoga professional, I thought I'd get one of my favorite Yoga chicks to chime in. This is in Fran Lewbel's words:

Ashtanga? Kundalini? Restorative? Bikram? Anasura? To name a few of the Yoga venues. Just the thought of picking is stressful enough to stop me in my Yoga pants.

How does Yoga fit in a world of cell phones, texting, P90X, triathlons, hip hop, dieting, waking up, going to bed, working, parenting, dating, drinking, partying, family, working out, stressing out...Why Yoga? Why the hype?

It was 1998, in my late 30's, when I took my first Yoga class. I had twelve years in the mortgage business, three years owning a coffee and bagel restaurant, two babies at home and pregnant with my 3rd son, PTA president, jog a thons, singing gigs, you know the type. I thought perhaps Yoga might help me calm myself. I felt like a hamster and there wasn't a wheel big enough.

In the beginning Yoga felt forced in a way. I would close my eyes and think, "I should be running, why am I here, I need to work out after this, what's for dinner?" I knew I needed the physicality of it; the strength and flexibility but I couldn't grasp the other stuff. I had too much mind chatter. The stories I had going on in my head about what was enough, were enough to make me crazy. What does that even mean?

A Yogini friend and fellow surf chick opened my eyes to other Yoga. Like anything else it's great to have a buddy. A friend who says, come on, lets just try it. The camaraderie in the fear of trying something new, in the embarrassment or the joy, is great to share with a friend. I tried different instructors, levels and venues and I began to find my place in Yoga. For me it was about finding a physically engaging class with an instructor who resonated with me. It's important to try new classes and teachers so you find a class that really appeals to you.

Ashtanga/Vinyasa flow Yoga became my mode of choice. The sequences improved my strength and flexibility and as I became familiar with the poses, gradually my mind began to quiet. The flow became a dance for me. The breath taking me into a pose and the exhale taking me out. I was settling in, becoming still in the mind and flow in my body. Soon my head was out of it. By that I mean, my head stopped judging. Can I lift my leg higher; do an extra push up in the chattaranga, cross my legs tighter? My body was on its own. Cues from teachers with reminders of the breath, and body movement, just came in without notice. I learned to stay in the moment and not think. In that I came to know that Yoga was enough.

The mind/body connection. The breath/body connection. The breath, body, mind and spirit connection. Yoga not only lengthens and strengthens the physical body but it does the same for the heart, head and spirit; whatever that may mean for you. It's a matter of taking the time to find the right class, and the right instructor who inspires you to find your connection with Yoga.

I start my own classes by reminding everyone to take their mind chatter and leave it outside the door. The hour we spend is about nurturing and taking care of ourselves. As for me, I tell myself that for the next hour in my one body I would like for everyone living in it to get along. So, on the awesome days when my Yoga practice brings my head, heart, body and spirit that much closer to togetherness, I have to say, "Namaste."

The various types of Yoga available are amazing. Try different instructors, levels and types of Yoga. Go online and there are plenty of free classes that you can watch and see what looks appealing. Here are a few:

Hatha Yoga- This type of Yoga is relatively slow paced, a gentle type of Yoga and is a good place to start if you are completely new to Yoga and don't know any of the asanas (poses). Like all types of Yoga, Hatha Yoga aims to unite the mind, body and spirit.

Ashtanga Yoga - This is the type of Yoga that I practice on a regular basis and means "eight limbs" in Sanskrit. It's a fast moving, intense style of Yoga practice and is based on a progressive set sequence of asanas, synchronized with the breath. Ashtanga Yoga can be quite physically demanding as you constantly move from one asana in the sequence to the next, so you'll find that it will improve your stamina as well as your flexibility and strength.

Power Yoga - This is a western interpretation of Yoga and is based on Ashtanga Yoga. A Power Yoga class may not necessarily stick to the exact sequence of poses like Ashtanga Yoga does, but it does involve practicing a series of poses without stopping and starting.

Iyengar Yoga - This type of Yoga is based on teachings by B.K.S Iyengar and concentrates on the correct alignment and form of the body. Unlike Ashtanga Yoga, there is an emphasis on holding each pose for a long period of time rather than moving constantly from one pose to the next. Iyengar Yoga uses props such as blocks and straps to help align the body into the different poses.

Vinyasa Yoga - Vinyasa means breath synchronized movement and is another fast paced type of Yoga, with an emphasis on breathing. A practice typically starts with sun salutations and moves on to more intense stretching. Throughout the practice each pose is balanced with a counter pose.

Bikram Yoga- Otherwise known as "Hot Yoga" is practiced in a room heated to 105 degrees, with a humidity of around 40%. Generally a sequence of 26 different poses is practiced during a Bikram Yoga class and the hot temperature helps to loosen muscles. Due to the high temperature most people sweat a lot during the class and this helps to cleanse the body of toxins.

I hope you enjoyed this brief exploration of Yoga and find a way to fit it into your life.

Exercise

Speaking of Tai Chi and Yoga, I wanted to address exercise as a stress-reducer. We all know we have to exercise for our bodies, but consider what it does for our minds. Exercise releases endorphins and other feel good hormones in the brain. It usually leads to better sleep. It is a moving meditation, especially something like running, swimming or walking. And there is no reason you can't throw an affirmation in while you're doing it. It gives us a better personal body image and often when we start doing things that are healthy, other unhealthy things drop away as well. After running 10 miles and feeling great, we are less apt to want to pig out on chocolate cake. Exercise has been known to decrease depression also. Regular exercise also helps condition the immune system so we stay healthier. Many people daydream during exercise and find with their minds clearer, they can come up with solutions to problems and options for their issues. And exercise itself seems to act as a buffer against stress.

The most important thing about exercise is to find what works best for you! Some people run, swim, walk, golf, surf, soccer, volleyball, badminton, the list is endless. I choose to dance. Dance not only strengthens my body, but it keeps my mind sharp and healthy. And it's good for my spirit. In fact a recent study on life satisfaction, showed that people who dance, have more life satisfaction that most other exercise.

To add in exercise, first off, pick something that you will enjoy. Start out slowly and be gentle with yourself. Get others to do it with you. Schedule it in so you know you have time for it. Change it up if you think you will get bored with one thing. And set realistic goals. You'll find as you reach them you'll be even more inspired to continue.

Thoughts from TJ Fortuna of Fortuna Fitness (my personal trainer).

Movement can play a major role in your effort to minimize stress levels in the body. I have clients that have been removed from benzodiazepines, otherwise known as "stress/anxiety reducing" medication, after adopting Tai Chi as a daily practice. Many times I have experienced clients tell me within a short span of 10 minutes of practice they feel relief and a weight lifted off of their shoulders. It appears that an increased awareness of breath work and purpose-filled movement has a positive impact on stress reduction.

When prescribing exercise to one of my clients, I look at all the other stressors in their life, and prescribe movement that balances the distress or negative stressors and eustress or positive stressors. This is important because although the body releases endorphins during exercise, too much exercise like, 60 minutes of high-intensity cardio 5-6 days a week, when improperly prescribed, can fry your adrenal system and add to the problem. When a client has demonstrated to me that they are under an enormous amount of stress already, I choose exercises that energize the body.

Exercise has two main categories; exercises that put energy in the body and exercises that take energy from the body. Soft Yoga, slow walks and tai chi are examples of exercise that energize the body. If you are under a high amount of stress already, these are a great place to start. Once you start incorporating energizing movement into your daily routine, you will experience a parasympathetic (healing/building) stress response that will boost your immune system, aid in balancing blood sugar, and slow down the aging process.

TJ Fortuna, personal trainer, fitness business consultant
www.tjfortuna.com

Herbs for Stress

Herbs were one of the first alternative health modalities that I was drawn to and so I was very excited when I first moved to California and found a bulk herb store down the street from me. I bought bags of herbs and made capsules, tinctures and teas. What I didn't realize though is that just because herbs are natural that doesn't mean they don't have side effects, dangers or interactions. For example, did you know that St. Johns Wort, commonly used for depression could counteract the birth control pill? So, your depression is gone until you get the pregnancy test results back. Anyway, I read in my herb book that horseradish was good for sinus problems. I had sinus problems and I had no idea what horseradish was. I bought powdered horseradish, made it into capsules and took some. SIX! A gallon of milk later to stop the burning...I realized that I had taken too much. So, the next day I tried it again. FOUR. Still not a great idea. I gave up on my horseradish experiment and to this day don't even think of offering me any with my prime rib. Aside from the blatant stupidity I mention above, please remember that herbs do interact with other things. If you want to use these herbs please consult with a professional or at the very least do some intense research, especially if you are taking prescriptions. First off, here are the common ways to take herbs.

-Capsule: Gelatin capsule containing powdered or chopped herbs that are often unpleasant to take directly by mouth. Most commercial herbs are given this way.

-Compress: A pad or cotton dipped in herbs that have been boiled in water. Good for swelling, pain, etc.

-Infusion: Pouring hot liquid over the herb and steeping; basically tea.

-Poultice: Warm mashed or ground herbs and applied directly to the skin.

-Tincture: Another common way to find commercially prepared herbs this involves soaking the herbs in an alcohol base and then straining them and taking the liquid by mouth or externally. This is a convenient way to take the herbs and they have a long shelf life with this preparation. You can also buy herbs in bulk and make your own tinctures.

Here are some herbs for stress:

Licorice Root contains a natural hormone alternative to cortisone, which can help the body handle stressful situations, and can help to normalize blood sugar levels as well as your adrenal glands, providing you with the energy necessary to deal with the stressful situation at hand. Among its many medicinal benefits, licorice is considered an adrenal tonic; in particular, it increases production of the very chemicals that aid in the body's recovery from chronic anxiety and stress.

Passionflower is considered a mild sedative and can help promote sleep. Passionflower also treats anxiety, insomnia, depression and nervousness.

Kava Kava, an herb from the South Pacific, is a powerful muscle relaxer and analgesic. Kava Kava is also effective at treating depression and anxiety associated with menopause.

St. John's Wort has been used medicinally since Hippocrates time. St. John's Wort has been the subject of many studies pitting it against prescription antidepressants. Many studies show it helps, many don't. I know multiple people who get relief from this common herb. St. John's Wort is most often taken as a capsule or tablet. It is often combined with valerian root when insomnia or restlessness are accompanying symptoms. St John's Wort works in two different ways to help with stress, it helps remove the stress hormone norepinephrine and also by creating the space for the pituitary gland to produce extremely beneficial hormones which go on to do much more good all through your systems. But don't forget it can interfere with the effectiveness of your birth control pill.

Lavender is the workhorse of herbs. It is effective at reducing irritability and anxiety, promoting relaxation, a sense of calm and sleep. It is also a powerful anti-bacterial agent, and can work to balance hormones and stimulate the immune system. While lavender can be consumed in a tea, it may work best as an essential oil that is breathed in by way of a diffuser or, in the case of stress and sleeplessness, an eye pillow. See page 111 on aromatherapy.

There is also a type of plant called an adaptogen. This helps the body adapt and deal with stress. Common adaptogens are ginseng, eleuthero and ashwagandha.

BEST

Linda Croyle BEST Master practitioner wrote this section. I was privileged to have a session by Linda and she is a featured guest on my TV series. Enjoy her information about this fascinating technique.

Bio Energetic Synchronistic Technique, or B.E.S.T., is a neuro-emotional process that addresses the mind, body, and spirit and their integrated influence on health. Developed more than 30 years ago by Dr. M.T. Morter Jr. (www.morter.com) and used across the globe, B.E.S.T. is a non-forceful energy balancing procedure used to bring the body and mind back into their natural alignment, which allows true health, and healing to take place. It is based on the belief that anything can be healed once we discover and remove the root interference or cause.

The Benefits of B.E.S.T.:
* *Creates a natural re-balancing of nervous system function*
* *Gentle, painless non-force method*
* *Addresses cause instead of symptoms*
* *Allows for healing without use of drugs, surgery, or other techniques with undesirable side effects*
* *Corrects nervous system function that could be hiding other problems that have not yet become symptomatic*

I use BEST to get at the underlying cause of a client's chronic illness or condition and/or to help remove the interference that's not allowing them to heal either physically or emotionally. For example, I had a client who had suffered from migraines for over 20 years. During one of our sessions, I asked him to recall his earliest memories of having migraines. He told me that they started happening when he was around 8 or 9 years old. When I asked him what would happen when he got them back then, he thought for a moment, then said, "My mother would pick me up and rock me in the rocking chair until they went away." When I asked if she would do this with him any other time, his face fell and he answered, "No." His unconscious brain had figured out that the best way to get some TLC was to have a migraine! We addressed this issue in the treatment (separated his need for TLC with migraines) and his migraines stopped that day!

People wanting more information on B.E.S.T., including how to become a B.E.S.T. Practitioner, can go to www.morter.com.

Traditional Chinese Medicine

Acupuncture and TCM are something I learned about in school, but is not in any way my area of expertise. So, I called in a pro. The following is from Lori Guynes, another guest on my show and a great friend.

Traditional Chinese Medicine (TCM) is excellent at addressing the effects of stress on emotional, physical and mental health. Internal or external factors can disrupt the natural flow of qi (vital life force energy) in the body. These stressors can also create imbalance of the yin and yang energies of the body. Yin relates to the cooling, resting, receptive energy and yang is connected to movement, warmth and action.

Stress impacts everyone differently, therefore the resulting pattern/s of imbalance will manifest in unique ways. There is not one standard diagnosis or treatment principle for the effects of stress in TCM. This is true for the medicine in general. Ten people can come in with the same Western diagnosis - such as Diabetes - but all ten individuals may receive varying TCM diagnoses and acupuncture, herbal and nutritional protocols.

With that being said, there are some common themes that emerge in relation to stress. The main organs/channels (referring to the energetic systems, not the literal organs) affected are the Heart and Liver.

In TCM, the Heart is said to house the spirit ("shen"). The blood nourishes the spirit, which is a yin substance. Constant stress or nutritional insufficiency can deplete the blood and yin and weaken Heart energy. This can manifest as fear, anxiety, depression, palpitations or sleep disorders.

When there is stagnation of qi (or heat or phlegm) then the mind/emotions will be agitated. With the excess in the Heart, a person may be overly excited or daring and be loud in speech and laughter. They may also have sleep issues, especially nightmares or excessive dreaming.

The Liver is the second energetic organ system most affected by stress. The liver is responsible for the free flow of energy throughout the body. When this flow gets stagnant due to a sedentary lifestyle, lack of emotional expression or poor eating habits, then the entire system feels stressed. In fact, pain is considered to be due to stagnation of qi/energy (or blood). Some of the common ways that stuck liver energy manifests is PMS, irritability, depression, muscle tension, headaches, allergies, eye issues, and indigestion.

One can help keep liver energy in healthy flow through moderate exercise and by not bottling up emotions, especially anger, resentment or frustration. Diet also plays a key role. Pesticides and other chemicals, alcohol, coffee (including decaffeinated), fried or fatty foods, and excess nuts can gum up the works. Certain foods and beverages can benefit liver health such as hot lemon water (especially in the morning) green leafy vegetables, beets and radishes.

Chinese medicine is based on the Taoist philosophy that human beings are microcosms of the natural environment and that we are seeking homeostasis - the balance of yin and yang energies.

It is important to notice if we lean on the side of being too yang - pushing, striving, doing. What kind of exercise do you do? Kickboxing, running, weight lifting, lots of intense cardio? Are you in constant motion? Eating on the go, multi-tasking.... Do you tend to like spicy foods?

Both the Heart and Liver benefit from calming lifestyle habits like meditation, yoga, tai chi, and deep belly breathing. These activities strengthen the yin and are calming to the nervous system.

If someone is lacking in yang energy, they may retain weight and experience lethargy, lack of motivation and lack of activity. This could be the classic "couch potato". It is possible that in response to stress, one can freeze or feel overwhelmed. Such a person could benefit from more movement and expression.

Acupuncture moves stagnant energy and redistributes the qi to where it is needed, therefore creating balance in the system. There are also Chinese herbs that nourish the yin, yang and blood, calm the shen/spirit, circulate the liver and so on. You can also use self-massage/acupressure of acupuncture points to help balance the Heart and Liver energies and to deal with stress.

Ren 17 - on the sternum/breast bone, at the fourth intercostal space, between the nipples. This can build energy and calm the emotions.

Yin Tang - on the forehead, between the eyebrows. Relaxing (and benefits eyes and sinus).

Pericardium 6 - on the inside of the forearm, about two inches up from the wrist, between the tendons. This is the point one would place "travel bands" for motion sickness treatment. This point both calms the heart and circulates the liver energy. As you probably guessed, it also treats nausea.

Liver 3 - on top of the foot, between the big toe and second toe (between the 1st and 2nd metatarsal bones), about an inch or two from the web, moving towards the leg. Great for moving the liver qi.

-------Lori Guynes, L.Ac., is a California licensed and nationally certified acupuncturist practicing in Santa Barbara, CA. She enjoys treating patients for stress and other health issues, and teaching them simple lifestyle and dietary changes that have a big impact.
www.Naturalreproductivehealth.com

Auditing

A naturopath named Jody, who I met at the American Naturopathic Medical Association conference the first year I attended, introduced me to Dianetic Auditing. He was doing an extra workshop on something called "assists." The theory behind assists is, let's say you hit your head and have pain. Immediately after you hit your head, go to where it happened and recreate it in the same place with the same object using very light touch, barely even making contact. The pain goes away. It really does. As he was giving us this talk I realized that someone had done this on me when I was in a play and a piece of the set fell on my head. She had the crew lift the piece and lean it over to tap my head in the exact same spot over and over until the pain was gone. I had no bruise, no headache, and no pain whatsoever. I raised my hand and shared that experience and I've been using assists since then. Jody and I became fast friends.

The following year he was doing another special lecture on auditing. This is basically the same thing as assists, but erases emotional trauma called "engrams."

Here's how it works; let's say that you were bit by a dog as a kid. Now, as an adult, any time you see a dog running toward you your heart races, you feel nauseous, get nervous and want to cry (called misemotion). That is not a realistic reaction to every dog running at you. Logically you know this isn't the same dog and you can reason that this dog isn't necessarily going to bite you, but somewhere in your brain, you see it as the same thing and have a physical reaction. Auditing has you tell your original story over and over again, adding more and more detail each time and eventually (like touching the object to my head over and over), the emotional event becomes a regular memory like anything else and doesn't carry that strong emotional charge. The next time you see a dog, the exaggerated reaction won't be there anymore.

It is also great for addressing physical pain as sometimes lasting aches and pains are stuck in the body from past trauma. It is pretty remarkable how it works.

More information can be found at www.dianetics.org and a DVD/book kit can be purchased at any Dianetics Center or on that website.

Past-Life Regression Therapy

Though something you might not think of as a mind/body technique, past-life regression therapy does utilize the mind/body connection to heal. It's best described by Peter Wright, a regression therapist.

In Past-Life Regression Therapy, we use a light hypnotic trance to take you back to an earlier time, whenever that time may be, in order to retrieve memories (e.g. one or more past-life stories) that may still be negatively influencing your present life and that are probably the source of your current symptoms. You are then encouraged to allow the story that emerges to unfold as if it is important. We then look for the "defeats" that you suffered and then help you come to closure with those who defeated you by confronting them, speaking your truth about what happened and then forgiving them if you were the victim. Or we seek forgiveness from those you harmed if you were the perpetrator in that "past-life story." By reaching closure with the other "characters" in your past-life story by apologizing to them directly for what you did, it is often much easier to forgive yourself for the part that you played in that "story." In short, since you have already expressed your remorse to them, they most likely have forgiven you. This often creates the healing of the issue in your current life.

Talk Therapy focuses on working with the ego and the conscious mind. Using a "past-life story" as the focal point, Past-Life Regression focuses not only on the mental subtle body, but also on the other subtle bodies that make up who we are: namely the physical subtle body, the emotional subtle body and the spirit body. With the help of the past-life story, <u>Regression Therapy can release trauma in the body, mind, emotions and spirit simultaneously.</u>

Benefits of Past-Life Regression Therapy
- *Faster and more concentrated than traditional forms of therapy*
- *Several issues can be worked on together*
- *Ego is not threatened – because you are just "telling" a story*
- *Experiential versus intellectual*
- *Discover that death is not an end*
- *Holistic – you are healing your mind, body and spirit all at once*

-Peter Wright, CPLT, CHT, LBLT
www.insightsfromwithin.com

I had the privilege of studying with the late Roger Woolger when I was in college. He regressed the entire group I was in and then picked select people with whom to do therapy. He guided the person through a past lifetime and then to the moment of death. What was significant at the moment of death were the thoughts and beliefs held at that time. Once these were defined, he took the person through death and to the "in between place" where the thoughts and beliefs could be processed. One example I remember was a woman who had current life issues with being overly attached and concerned for her children. It was discovered during Past Life Regression Therapy that in a former life, she had died young and felt that she had abandoned her family. At her moment of death, she was guilty, angry and scared. She worked through those feelings with Roger and afterwards found that her reaction in this life was healthier towards her children. Just like many of the modalities I have mentioned in this book, Past-Life Regression Therapy also deals with past trauma and thought patterns, but perhaps on a deeper level.

One doctor had asked Roger, "What if we were just making this all up? What if it's fiction and there's no such thing as past lives?" His response, "Who cares where it actually comes from. Whatever story comes forward is clearly the story that must be told to get to the root of the issue. Whether true past life, or made up fiction, it is helping the person deal with the issue." More information about Roger Woolger's techniques and philosophies can be found at www.deepmemoryprocess.com. His technique, Deep Memory Process, combines active imagination, bodywork and psychodrama with shamanic/spiritual journeying and integration between lifetimes a la The Tibetan Book of the Dead. Though Roger passed away in 2011 there are teachers around the globe that are still carrying on his legacy with teaching and counseling.

Another example of healing through past life therapy is with the books of Yale trained physician, Dr. Brian Weiss. The most popular is *Many Lives, Many Masters*. Dr. Weiss was taken aback when one of his patients Catherine returned to past lives under hypnosis. There was a big connection between her relationships now and then and her ailments and phobias in this life and past lives. As he helped counsel her through the other lives, the pain and issues in her current life cleared away. A recent gallop poll indicates that 20% of Americans believe in past lives.
http://en.wikipedia.org/wiki/Reincarnation

According to all these experts, it doesn't even matter if you believe. The story that must be told will be told. More information about Dr. Weiss can be found at www.brianweiss.com.

Rolfing

Rolfing, also known as Structural Integration, is a healing technique created by Ida Rolf that alleviates restriction in the joints and muscles, resulting in increased mobility. I wanted to include Rolfing because many people think it's a massage technique, but in reality it is its own system of healing with training taking twelve to eighteen months to complete. I believe Rolfing is relevant to the field of mind/body because the body remembers emotional trauma and holds onto it in patterns. Often during Rolfing, memories come to the surface and the client may have an emotional or energetic release. I've had this happen with clients during basic massage as well, but with Rolfing, emotional and energetic release is much more expected, and part of the healing process. Rolfing is usually done in ten sessions with a different section of the body being worked in each session. Rolfing releases restriction in joints and muscles for freer unrestrictive movement. There are also movement sessions that are incorporated to eliminate bad patterns and allow you to walk, stand, sit and move in a different way. Often our movement patterns are already ingrained by childhood and may actually reflect our thought processes and emotional issues. Rolfing Movement Integration is purported to help restructure these physical-emotional connections into more healthy patterns. For more information about Rolfing training and to find a practitioner visit www.rolf.org.

Out of Rolfing came a system called Soma Neuromuscular Integration. More information can be found at http://www.soma-institute.org/.

Hanna Somatic Education

Hanna Somatic Education (HSE), founded by Thomas Hanna, is based on the work of Hans Selye, who recognized the role of stress in disease and Moshe Feldekrais, who had his own healing system. This system is based on three reflexes: the startle response, Landau arousal response and the trauma reflex. Each of these reacts with different muscular stress responses in the body like closing the eyes, contracting the head back or engaging the muscles to flee. Over time, repeated responses form patterns in the muscles that are exacerbated to the point where we can no longer voluntarily relax the muscles. This results in loss of range of motion and pain. This HSE system uses hands-on work and movement re-education. Hanna believed that as these physical patterns are eliminated, so are the psychological habits. More information and cds outlining these techniques can be found at http://hannasomatics.com/.

Body/Mind Centering

Body-Mind Centering (BMC) by Bonnie Bainbridge Cohen focuses on the intimate connection of how the mind is expressed through the body. According to this system, just as we can feel movement in our body like our arm, we can develop sensation of any organ and system and change it if need be. BMC also associates a state of mind with each tissue in the body. This method combines hands on, movement, guided imagery, pictures, dialogue, music and more. I've never had any experience with this modality, but from what I've read it appears to be a pretty thorough technique in assisting people with illnesses connected to mind/body. This system requires extensive training, 1000+ hours in four terms over four years as well as an optional Teacher Certification Program. More information can be found at http://www.bodymindcentering.com.

Polarity Therapy

Randolph Stone who was an osteopath, naturopath, chiropractor and versed in reflexology, Chinese medicine and Ayurveda created Polarity Therapy. He viewed humans as energetic being and believed energy flowed between negative and positive poles in the body. According to Polarity Therapy, there are five vertical currents that flow up the body on the front and back, and each corresponds to a certain chakra, element or life function. There are horizontal zones of energy as well. A block anywhere in the energy currents results in physical and emotional imbalance.

A Polarity Therapy practitioner accesses the energy currents and then using hands-on positions unblocks and balances the energy. The pressure of the hands vary and sometimes the hands do not touch the body at all, but only interact with the energy field above the body. Founder Randolph Stone believed that once the life force was in balance, physical ailments would balance as well. After a session with a practitioner, the client would then be given instruction for cleansing diets, polarity yoga and changing negative thought patterns. I remember when I learned this in my basic massage classes, it was one of my favorites and very effective for pain relief. More information can be found at http://www.polaritytherapy.org.

Zero Balancing

Zero Balancing (ZB), created by Fritz Frederick Smith, MD is another system of energy and the body. It, like Polarity Therapy, is done fully clothed and involves manipulation of the energy by a practitioner. The practitioner will scan the energy field and then move energy by manipulating the body. Practitioners closely monitor the client by observing reactions such as breath and facial expressions. Smith believes that the tissues of the body hold emotions; memory, past experiences, etc. and that by using ZB you can override those vibrations. The vibration will get released which causes an expanded state of consciousness. This is a system of stress reduction and reprogramming. Certification has multiple requirements including 100 hours of class, receiving sessions, performing sessions and writing papers. More information can be found at http://www.zerobalancing.com.

Therapeutic Touch

Dolores Krieger and her teacher Dora Kunz popularized Therapeutic Touch. It's a contemporary modification of the ancient art of laying on hands. This is appropriate, as is Reiki, for someone who can't have massage or for whom it would be painful. This system works on the aura, which is the energy field that surrounds the body.

A session is done in five steps; first the practitioner centers themselves to become clear and focused; then for a period of up to twenty five minutes, the practitioner acts as a human energy support system by holding one palm facing the back of the body and one facing the front, about three inches away to access the energy field of the client. He moves his hands up and down the body scanning the energy and looking for cues about the energy distribution. He assesses if there is a hot or cold spot, thickness, pressure, emptiness, etc.

Step three consists of clearing those discovered spots and balancing that energy using a series of sweeping hand movements down the person's energy field. In step four harmony is established by toning down excess energy or strengthening vital energy if it is low. This is not done on the physical plane, but in the mind of the practitioner. For example, if he finds a cold spot he can visualize what it was like to feel warm and send that image to the client. Color correspondences can also be used.

Step five involves "unruffling" any turbulence in the client's field and smoothing out wrinkles. This is accomplished by moving the hands outward and progressing from the head to the feet. The Therapeutic Touch (TT) technique does not attempt to cure disease, but rather stimulates the natural healing process.

Over thirty years of clinical experience and research in TT shows that TT can decrease pain, induce profound relaxation, promote rest and sleep, lessen anxiety and accelerate wound healing. TT can also have an effect on psychological and spiritual levels. TT focuses on healing rather than curing and has benefits unique to each person. I also know a lot of TT practitioners work on animals.

More information can be found at
http://www.therapeutictouch.org.

Chi Kung

Chi Kung or Qi Gong translates to "working with life energy" or "breathing skill."[76] This moving form of meditation, which looks very similar to Tai Chi, strengthens the immune system and heals on a deep level of body, mind and soul. It embodies the essence of chi, animates the human organism and connects us to the air, food and environment in which we live. The deep breathing vitalizes tissues and organs, bones and muscles. It relieves pain, eliminates stress and emits chi to heal others. It has also been shown to help with high blood pressure and cancer. It's estimated that 80 million people practice daily in China. It helps with a calm spirit and peaceful mind so one is more capable of dealing with daily life. Practitioners can also use Qi Gong to heal others by scanning their chi and projecting healing chi to any areas that are deficient or out of balance. Many studies have been done on the benefits of this healing art. The website for the Qi Gong Institute offers DVDs, books, articles and a plethora of other information about this fabulous art.

http://www.qigonginstitute.org

---

[76] Knaster, M. *Discovering the Body's Wisdom.* Bantam Publishing. New York. 1996.

Rubenfeld Synergy Method

This is a system of alternative medicine that combines touch and talk to help people deal with stress. It uses the body as a starting point knowing that many emotions are stored and expressed through the physical.

A session occurs with the client fully clothed lying down or sitting in a chair. The practitioner begins by inviting the client to notice and express any feelings or thoughts. They then make gentle contact with the body, often beginning at your head or feet. There is sharing of what the client is sensing and experiencing at each point of contact. This process can lead to new experiences of awareness, self-discovery and deep emotional connection.

There are basic principles of this practice as noted at www.rubenfeldsynergy.com:

-Each individual is unique
-The mind, body, emotions and spirit are dynamically connected
-Awareness is the key to change
-Change can only occur in the present even if your stressors are coming from the past or future
-The ultimate responsibility lies with the client
-We have the natural capacity for self-healing and self-regulation
-The body's energy field and life force not only exist but also can be sensed
-Touch is a form of communication
-The body is a metaphor and may represent emotional issues
-The body tells the truth and is guided by the body's message
-The body is the sanctuary for the soul
-Pleasure needs to be supported to balance pain
-Humor can lighten and contribute to health

-Reflecting clients' verbal expressions validate the experience
-Confusion facilitates change
-Altered states of consciousness can enhance healing
-Integration is necessary for lasting results

This looks like a fabulous modality, which incorporates so much of what we've talked about in this book. There is a wealth of information on the website along with some helpful videos about the practice.

To become a practitioner you must go through the training, which is a twelve-week/twelve weekend intensive program spread over a four-year period. This model allows trainees to continue with their professional lives while they complete the training, thereby making it accessible to a wide and diversified group. Class attendees have included physicians, massage therapists, physical therapists, psychotherapists, nurses, and even actors, musicians, and business executives. Trainees must actually experience the Rubenfeld Synergy Method, so they are required to participate in twenty private sessions a year with a Rubenfeld practitioner. Graduate practitioners are referred to as Certified Rubenfeld Synergists®.

SHEN

SHEN Physio-Emotional Relief Therapy merges the concept of how emotion works with the physics of the biofield or chi. It is a therapy developed over twenty-five years ago by Richard Pavek and is a process of emotional unfolding, de-layering and growth. It's described as an updated version of ancient hands-on healing techniques. It uses the low level electromagnetic field (biofield) to resolve chronic pain and emotional issues.

As described on the www.shentherapy.info website, SHEN *works like this: using the biofield (chi from our hands), we first loosen the contractions trapping the painful emotions deep inside the body, then we reposition our hands to lift the emotions to the surface where they can dissipate. This process is repeated as necessary and sets the stage for a sound, positive emotional shift. Once the old painful emotions have been dissipated, the deeper empowering emotions of confidence, joy and love are freed to establish a robust, resilient emotional core upon which to shift one's life.*

To me, it seems quite similar to many other hands-on healing techniques, working with chi to effect change in the physical body. Getting certified is quite a process involving joining the organization, 686 hours minimum of study and internship program and completing 200 hours of client sessions. After that you basically petition to be certified including writing papers about your own shortcomings and how you expect to overcome them and speak of your own guilt, fear and shame. This is an interesting technique, but I honestly wonder if it's any different than other energy techniques that aren't as strict with their certification process. I'm open to anything though and if it speaks to you...go for it!

Jin Shin Do

"Jin Shin Do" means "The Way of the Compassionate Spirit." Jin Shin Do® Bodymind Acupressure® classes teach the use of gentle yet deep finger pressure on specific acupoints and verbal Body Focusing techniques, to help release "armoring" or chronic tension, balance the Chi, and improve vitality. This clothes-on method helps relieve stress and trauma-related problems. A unique synthesis of a traditional Japanese acupressure technique, classic Chinese acupuncture and acupressure theory, Taoist philosophy, Qigong (breathing and exercise techniques), Reichian segmental theory and principles of Ericksonian psychotherapy. Originated by psychotherapist **Iona Marsaa Teeguarden**, JSD promotes a pleasant trancelike state, in which one can relax and move out of the head and into the body, accessing feelings and inner wisdom.

The JSD acupressurist holds combinations of acupoints. Initial sensitivity at the points is soon replaced by a pleasurable feeling of release. The work is characterized by non-invasiveness, safety in touch, and a sense of wonder and synchronicity. The client may share feelings or emotions that surface during the release of tension and stress, or just relax, perhaps falling into a deep and refreshing sleep. The JSD acupressurist evaluates the tension pattern through point palpation and pulse reading, then holds successive "local points" in tense or painful areas together with related "distal points," which help the tension to release more easily, deeply and pleasantly. Points are held approximately one to three minutes. Classes range from two-fourteen hours by certified instructors. As described at http://www.jinshindo.org.

EFT

EFT or Emotional Freedom Technique (also know as tapping or meridian tapping) is a system of using the fingers to stimulate places on the body to relieve stress. It is a combination of ancient Chinese acupressure and modern psychology. It was developed originally by Roger Callahan in the 1980s and modified and expanded upon by Gary Craig. This simple technique, which literally involves "tapping" on the meridian points of our body while saying certain statements, provides uniquely powerful results. There are spots on the face, which experts point out, that we naturally touch during stress or anxiety. They are also found on the pinky side of the hand and spots under the clavicles. It is believed that by stimulating these points with tapping, the stress response is decreased. This technique is used frequently for veterans with PTSD and the population at large to help them deal with stress. There is a specific pattern of the points that are stimulated while saying a repeated phrase. A worksheet from their website explains the steps:

1. Where in the body are you feeling the stress?
2. Determine the stress level on a scale of 1 to 10.
3. Tap the side of the hand while repeating, "Even though I have _____ (name problem), I deeply and completely accept myself."
4. Do the tapping sequence consisting of points on the chest and face.
5. After you've done that determine the new stress level and if it's still high, repeat the process.

More can be seen at http://www.eftuniverse.com where they not only have the have the history and training required to do EFT, but also a very informative videos. I found this technique to be intriguing and look forward to learning more.

Breath Work/Rebirthing

Yoga, Tai Chi and many other somatic modalities concentrate on the breath for healing. It is very apparent when we are stressed that we breathe more shallowly. When we are startled we have a sharp intake of air and when we are relieved, we let out a big sigh. Even in the mind/body realm, we have phrases like:

> Don't hold your breath
> Breathe a sigh of relief
> Breathe easy

I did a few sessions of rebirthing with my Reiki Master where I lay on the table and breathed deeply and rapidly for almost an hour. I found it interesting and invigorating, and walked away clearer if not a bit light-headed. This breathing technique helps activate and release stored stress, pain and emotional trauma and brings about change by reversing "limiting beliefs" that tend to block our ability to change. It works with a process of "conscious centered breathing" or the "circular breath." It is recommended that you work with a trainer or coach who can lead you to deeper issues and support your process.

Another breath technique I found is Biodynamic Breath Therapy, which uses Trance Energetic Breathing. From what I understand, this is very similar to rebirthing and uses the technique of breathing through the mouth without pausing between inhales and exhales. The breathing technique is accompanied by touch and bodywork. For more information see their website www.biodynamicbreath.com.

Autogenic Training

Autogenic training can trace its roots back to the German psychiatrist, Johannes Heinrich Schultz in 1932. It is very similar to Progressive Muscle Relaxation where you tense and then relax muscles in a pattern to induce deeper relaxation. It differs, however, in that it also works with weight and temperature. It is described as taking considerable time and discipline to learn and the site I found suggested that it takes over three months to master. I have used these techniques in a minimal way with clients, asking them to picture a limb or body part as heavy and warm. Autogenics means "self-produced" and this is considered a self-care method.

It is begun with a breathing warm-up where you inhale for a certain duration and exhale twice as long. Start out with a one-count inhalation and a two-count exhalation and increase the time until you get to six on the inhale. Reverse until you are back to one. For example, inhale one, exhale two, inhale two, exhale four, inhale three, exhale six, etc. and then reverse. In the next step, you concentrate on your dominant arm and program that arm to get limp and heavy, then limper and heavier, etc. This step should be done two-three times daily for three days. This process continues for weeks until you have worked with all sections of the body including the heart, breath and stomach. You use heat commands as well as weight.

Though time consuming, it is a fabulously relaxing technique that may be beneficial for you.
www.guidetopsychology.com/autogen.htm

EMDR

I wanted to include some information on EMDR or Eye Movement Desensitization and Reprocessing, but in doing some research, it seems more geared to very severe anxiety as found in PTSD and rape trauma. If you have experienced a traumatic life experience and are having trouble coping, this method may work for you. Below are some informational sites that you might find useful.

http://www.webmd.com/mental-health/emdr-what-is-it
http://www.emdr.com
http://www.emdria.org

NLP

NLP stands for Neuro-Linguistic Programming, a name that encompasses the three most influential components involved in producing human experience: neurology, language and programming. The neurological system regulates how our bodies function, language determines how we interface and communicate with other people and our programming determines the kinds of models of the world we create. Neuro-Linguistic Programming describes the fundamental dynamics between mind (neuro) and language (linguistic) and how their interplay affects our body and behavior (programming).

Founders Grinder and Bandler formalized their modeling techniques and their own individual contributions under the name "Neuro-Linguistic Programming" to symbolize the relationship between the brain, language and the body. Through the years, NLP has developed some very powerful tools and skills for communication and change in a wide range of professional areas including: counseling, psychotherapy, education, health, creativity, law, management, sales, leadership and parenting. From the site www.nlpu.com, with permission.

The following is taken from the site: http://www.nlpco.com. There you can find more information about NLP and their book, *NLP: The Essential Guide to Neuro Linguistic Programming.*

NLP is like the 'user's manual' for the mind, and allows us to use the language of the mind to consistently achieve our specific and desired outcomes. When you learn NLP, you learn specific skills and patterns necessary to make positive changes, create new choices, be more effective with others, break free of old habits, self-destructive patterns and behaviors, and think more clearly about what it is you want.

Body Talk

Body Talk, at its most basic, is a combination of muscle testing and tapping. A session takes anywhere from fifteen to forty-five minutes and is typically done fully clothed. Dr. Veltheim founded this system in the mid 1990s. It works with the widely believed theory that the body has innate wisdom of what is wrong and the ability to heal itself. Body Talk takes three initial approaches:

1. What is wrong
2. What links do we need to establish to fix it
3. And then tapping that change into the brain to normalize health patterns of the body

It can be learned in a day to deal with 50-60% of healthcare issues.

Body Talk relies on the body telling the practitioner of any communication circuits that may have been compromised and need to be reestablished. The practitioner uses the Body Talk Protocol Chart to determine what may need to be reconnected. The reconnection is done by touch and tapping. Very similar to tapping the "save" command on a computer keyboard, tapping on the head communicates to the brain to "save" the connection in the body that needs to be reconfigured. Tapping on the sternum is used to "save" the connection in the heart – information that is shared with every cell in the body. I have heard of numerous practitioners that use this system and many people recommended that I include it in the book. More information and some great videos can be found at http://www.bodytalksystem.com. There are numerous courses all over the world which can also be found on the website above.

Sound Healing

One of the most ancient ways to relax was with music: instruments, the voice, singing bowls, drums and tuning forks. Relaxing music is often played during massage sessions, but some music can be far more healing than others.

As a massage therapist, I am a big fan of Steven Halpern. His was one of the first CDs I played for massage and it's a standard for most people's practices. Steven Halpern differs from most "relaxing music" in that he often uses subliminal messages or certain tones and rhythms to deepen healing and relaxation. His music is based on resonance, entrainment and intention. You don't have to do anything but listen. He lists the benefits of sound healing as:

-Increased feelings of well being, happiness and inner peace
-Ease of falling asleep and waking up refreshed
-A more robust immune system
-Greater concentration, focus and creativity

More about Mr. Halpern and his music can be found at www.innerpeacemusic.com.

Hemi-Sync is another form of sound healing. I was introduced to this phenomenal system when I was having knee surgery. A friend gave me a series of tapes to play before, during and after surgery. They program the brain to assist the body. I wore headphones during the surgery and hit play as they were putting me under anesthesia. I instructed my nurse to change to the post-op tape when the surgery was over. I remember hearing, "You will now be fully awake, 5, 4, 3, 2, 1" and on one, I opened my eyes. I saw the nurse sitting next to me reading a magazine. I said, "Hi." very loudly and scared the daylights out of her. She startled and the magazine went flying, "I didn't expect you up for another 45 minutes." She said, "What are you listening to?"

In the Hemi-Sync system, the left and right hemispheres of the brain work together using different sound waves. For example, their sleep CD works mainly with delta frequencies and learning products use primarily beta waves. Though one frequency might be dominant, all frequencies are mixed together, which is the key to its effectiveness.

Hemi-Sync is similar to hypnosis in that it induces an altered state of mind in which the body is deeply relaxed. It is sometimes described as "focused concentration." Unlike Halpern's work, Hemi-Sync is not filled with subliminal messages. These tapes have worked for multiple surgeries I have had and I've used the pain management tapes with my clients with great results. I had one cancer sufferer who was having incredible pain. I would have her wear headphones with the pain tape during her Reiki sessions and she said it was one of the only times she wasn't suffering. More information about Hemi-Sync can be found at www.hemi-sync.com.

NET

NET, short for Neuro-Emotional Technique is a fascinating but complicated method. The website says you learn the basics and can start practicing after a weekend of training, but the explanations of how it all works are very scientific and I had trouble distilling it down to basics here. So, with their permission, I have included a selection of direct segments from their website http://www.netmindbody.com.

"Although we find stress to be a big component of health, it is very important to understand that any problem can include factors of the other bases [They use a baseball diamond for a visual], *and it is necessary to address all factors related to one's health.*

-1st base represents emotional or stress-related factors, and NET is one of the approaches used to help patients.

-2nd base represents the effects of toxins on the body (things that are in the body and should not be there). Specific homeopathic support can help many cases where there is a toxic condition. Drs. Scott and Deb Walker have developed a special line of NET Remedies® for patient support during the healing process.

-3rd base represents biochemistry or the nutrition factor of health (things that should be in the body and may be less than adequate). Diet and specific nutritional support may need to be addressed.

-4th base represents structural and physical corrections. This factor is addressed relative to the practitioner's field of expertise.

NET (neuro-emotional technique) is based on the physiological foundations of stress-related responses. As discovered in the late 1970s, emotional responses are composed of neuropeptides (amino acid chains) and their receptors, which lie on neurons and other cells of remote tissues in the body. The neuropeptides are ejected from the neuron and carry the encoded "information" to other sites within the body. These neuropeptides are in a category of neurochemicals known as Information Substances (IS). IS's are released at times of stress-related arousal and become attached to remotely-positioned neuroreceptors.

Significantly, this process also happens when a person recalls to memory an event in which a stress originally occurred. This is a key factor in the NET treatment. Thus, the physiological status of the body is emotionally replicating a similar physiological state that was found in the original conditioning event by the process of remembering.

Here's a classic example of how a physiological response can be associated with a memory: Visualize a lemon . . . go ahead . . . try it. Now, think about cutting into that lemon — smell the lemony scent and see the juice running down the sides of the lemon. Now, squeeze some of the lemon's juice into your mouth and take a big bite of the lemon. Is your mouth watering? If you're like most people, it is, and what you're experiencing is a physiological response to the memory of a lemon. The body's response to stress works in a similar way.

The conditioning process is based on the principles of the great physiologist Pavlov, who demonstrated that an organism can be physiologically stimulated by a previously ineffective stimulus. For example, a bell normally does not stimulate salivary secretion. However, a bell may stimulate salivary secretion if the animal has been conditioned by associating the sound of a bell with the sight or smell of meat.

Also, it is normal that after a time of having the bell ring with no food association, the secretion of saliva (a physiological process) will stop. This is known as extinction. If the physiology of the animal is out of balance at the time of conditioning, the normal process of extinction may not take place, thus allowing for recurrent stimulation and an aberrant physiology. These aberrations are called NECs.

Thus, if the body was in a low state of resistance at the time of a stressfully charged event and the event is recalled to (conscious/nonconscious) memory, this low state of physiological resistance will also be duplicated in the present-day body.

As an example, it has been observed that many patients who have been in automobile accidents are often slow to recover and fearful about driving for surprisingly varying lengths of time. The extinction process of the conditioning resulting from the automobile accident is very much individualized. While most patients may fret or be extra alert for a week or so after the accident, they usually return to a normal state. However, there are some patients who do not seem to fully recover from their conditioned responses and may be consciously or unconsciously driving in an extra-tense and highly vigilant state, with some to the point of not driving at all. This in part also answers the question of why two people in the same accident, sustaining similar injuries, can have a great disparity in recovery times."

So, there it is. I hope you found that description helpful. It looks to me like a really thorough mind/body technique and their website shares a vast amount of information. The website also states that NET works with emotional memory, not historical memory. In other words, how you perceived the event happening has far greater impact than how the event "really happened." That can be very useful when trying to erase the memories stored in the body. And this sounds remarkably similar to the philosophy of past life regression therapy.

You can check out research on NET and other mind/body studies on the following websites: www.netmindbody.com and http://www.onefoundation.org.

One More Thing

Throughout my research for this book, I came across tons of very similar modalities that could be added. I gave you descriptions of quite a few, but here are some others that were suggested to me that I just couldn't cover.

Silva Mind Control: http://www.silvamethod.com

Quantum Touch: http://www.quantumtouch.com

Ortho-bionomy: http://www.ortho-bionomy.org

Neuroliminal Training: http://neuroliminaltraining.com

DET (Direct Energy Transference): www.dettherapy.com

MVVT (Maharishi Vedic Vibration Technology): http://www.vedicvibration.com

Mind/Body Medicine for Pain Management

We have all felt pain, whether we hit our thumb with a hammer or woke up with a headache. Even though I mention pain throughout the book, I wanted to include a section on mind-body therapies for pain management as my background is in massage and helping people deal with their pain.

Pain is usually a signal that something is wrong. But some people find themselves having a chronic pain syndrome. There are also diseases and disorders like fibromyalgia, osteoarthritis and rheumatoid arthritis that can cause incredible pain in the body. We know that everyone perceives pain differently and everyone has a different pain tolerance or threshold. There are also theories that thoughts and emotions directly influence physiological responses like muscle tension, blood flow and levels of brain chemistry. It's also suggested that stressful thoughts lead to pain in vulnerable parts of the body as I mentioned previously.

Anticipation of pain can make it worse, for example if you start to feel a bad headache coming on, the stress of it hurting or what it's going to do to your day can actually make it worse. Avoiding things that we think may hurt us, can also indirectly cause pain by losing blood flow and muscle tone. The other thing we have to consider (which I mention later) is secondary gain. Is there something we're getting that is good from staying sick? Please look at any of Dr. Sarno's books for great insight into our emotions and pain. Here are some specific mind/body techniques for pain.

Depending on the type of pain, massage can be incredibly useful. Though in that case you would probably be using it strictly as a physical modality, it does calm and soothe the nervous system as well as smooth out muscle tension and help feel-good hormones in the brain erase that pain response.

Reiki is also good for pain and can be very good at connecting the mind and body and helping calm the emotions and spirit when chronic pain is present. It also can decrease pain. I had a friend visiting from Los Angeles who had twisted his ankle the day before. We were sitting in a bar with friends having a drink and he was complaining about the pain. I asked him to put his leg up on my mine and I put my hands on his ankle. I sent Reiki for about 15 minutes before he finally said, "Oh my God, what are you doing?!" He almost sounded angry and I thought I had hurt him. "I'm doing Reiki." I said. "Why, is it hurting?" "No, I don't feel it at all, all the pain is gone." He jumped up and started to walk on it. All the pain was gone. And as a reminder, you can do Reiki on yourself; many people I've trained weren't professionals but people who wanted it for their own personal life.

Meditation is a remarkable way of decreasing pain response. Multiple studies have been done showing that people who go into a meditative state register less pain in their brains. Whether you do full-blown sit on the pillow meditation or just minis a few times a day, it can help stop your pain.

Visualizing your pain is a wonderful way to help it go away. Whether you picture it as a large lump of ice that is melting, or a block of rock that your construction worker is chipping away at, or whether you see angels swooping into carried away, studies show that this type of visualization can actually decrease your pain level. One study I remember reading showed an AIDS patient visualizing a radio dial with his pain amount on it. He would then incrementally turn the dial so that it got lower and lower. And his pain actually decreased. We have to remember that programming our minds also programs our bodies.

Don't forget about affirmations for pain management also. Don't say, "I'm no longer in pain." Say, "My neck is stable and healthy."

As was shown in Benedetti's studies on open versus closed treatments, the placebo is incredibly useful in taking care of pain. I'm not telling you to have someone trick you into taking fake pain meds, but the theory behind it is always fascinating. The opiate receptors in the brain start to light up just at the beginning of the pain medication being distributed.

Anything at all that you can do to relax your body will help with your pain. Often when we are in pain we tighten up our muscles in response. This just causes a cyclical event of pain, tension, pain, tension. If you can relax your muscles your pain will decrease. Doing deep breathing, perhaps with some aromatherapy like lavender, can help decrease the pain response in the body. Deep breathing also gets oxygen into the muscles and the brain and can help with the pain. And sometimes just plain distraction can help.

Depending on what's causing your pain progressive muscle relaxation can be a great tool. This involves tensing of your feet as hard as you can, and then relaxing, then tensing your calf hard and then relaxing them, and working your way slowly up the body. And gentle movement like tai chi or Yoga can be great for stimulating both the body and mind and calming the nervous system. And don't forget getting therapies like hydrotherapy or PT.

There are so many non-allopathic ways to help pain; I've mentioned just some of them here. Please explore what works for you and don't feel trapped in a Western Medicine Model or feel like you have to suffer. You can take control and help yourself!

Things That Make Me Go Hmmmmmm...

I mention a lot of different techniques in this book. Some might resonate with you and others might seem too out there or weird. I'm not advocating one over the other. I'm simply offering options of what you might try. However, in my many years of experience I have been exposed to things that I feel are just plain hooey. The patches that drain all the toxins out of your feet? Yeah, those don't do anything. I'll share an experience at my first naturopath conference.

I was new at the conference and quite intimidated by older members that I wasn't even close to in experience or education and I went to the conference with the idea that I was going to try everything. A man was demonstrating ionic footbaths and there were about four people sitting in a circle with their feet in gunky water. I wanted to try it too. So I reluctantly gave him $20 and he filled my basin. He went on to explain to me how much money I could make in my practice after I bought my own unit and how great all the extra income would be.

As I sat, multiple people came up to buy their unit for the special price of $695. I was leery. The longer I sat with my feet in the basin, the darker and foamier the water became and soon there was a grey sludge forming on top that looked like soap scum. He walked over and said, "Oh, yeast." I questioned him. "Oh, clearly you have a candida overgrowth, that's what that is in the water." I said, "How is systemic candida coming out of my feet? That's physiologically impossible." He just looked at me.

Apparently I was the only one that questioned these things. I bent over to take some of the scum out of the water and look at it. He stopped me and said I didn't want to do that. Yes I did. I rubbed it between my fingers and asked if it could be residue from my shampoo, body wash, shaving cream, soap or sweat from being in shoes all day. "No...well, maybe a little." I finished my "treatment" and he wanted to know how many units I wanted to buy. I told him none. His response was, "Must be nice to not need $10,000 extra a month."

I was appalled, and scared. Was this alternative medicine? Part of the answer is yes. And it's things like that that give alternative therapies a bad name. There is a lot of crap out there. So when approached with the newest gadget or device or therapy, please explore what you are paying for. If the promise is a cure or a MLM system designed to make you tons of money, it might just be too good to be true. Do your research and follow your instincts.

I have also had clients that buy their own really expensive gizmos and rely so heavily on them that they lose their own sense of self and judgment. I'm sure when you are faced with a terminal illness or chronic pain that you'll try anything and everything. Unfortunately though, much of it is a waste of time and money. It's the old proverb, if it sounds too good to be true, it probably is.

Something else I've had mixed experience with is Applied Kinesiology or muscle testing. This technique, where you push down on a strongly held arm or leg to check for energetic strength in the body, can be used for everything from checking for illness, asking the body's preference for a treatment or looking for deficiencies that might need a supplement. Then you can muscle test the supplement or homeopathic. I've seen some amazing feats of muscle testing. Donna Eden, a well-known expert in energetic healing, has some excellent and authentic demonstrations of muscle testing on her DVDs.

I've also seen some really weird things. I was at a kinesiology workshop when a man answered his phone, talked to a client and proceeded to muscle test her over the phone using his own fingers to tell her how much of a certain supplement to take. Sorry folks, not buying it! I've seen people muscle test their produce in stores, which does make shopping a time consuming experience. I had a client come to my office and tell me she was having thyroid issues and was taking a lot of supplements for it. In my experience thyroid issues typically need hormonal intervention not a lot of supplements. I asked her what her blood test showed; she told me she didn't have one. I asked her how she knew her thyroid was off kilter. Her chiropractor had muscle tested her and it came up. He then sold her tons of expensive supplements. I sent her to my favorite endocrinologist for a blood test and there was absolutely nothing wrong with her thyroid. What was wrong was with her chiropractor. This is where I appreciate Western medicine. It has great diagnostics. Let's use them when we need to. For things that could easily and inexpensively be addressed with allopathic medicine, let's do it and leave the arm pushing for emotional/spiritual issues or actually testing muscles and organs.

I wanted to add a brief word about medical freedom here. I believe we should all have access to the kind of care we want and it sickens me that practitioners that are curing disease are being run off to other countries and have to skirt the law to save lives. The FDA recently banned ear candles. Seriously. Ear candles. With all the complaints about prescriptions and artificial sweetener and people dying everyday from bad drugs, they outlaw ear candles. If I want to have my ears coned I should be allowed. If I want to try some fringe cancer treatment, I should be allowed. And in the same way, if you want to put your feet in bubbly dirty water and you think it works, you should be allowed. Because just as I say that the ionic footbaths don't work, are a waste of money and total hokum, so someone else will say the same thing about homeopathics, ear candles, herbs for cancer and all the mind/body techniques I just shared with you. So, there is no easy solution to this right now. It's all or nothing. As one of my clients said, "There are good quacks and there are bad quacks and then the people that fall between the quacks." I guess I am the latter.

Attitude is Everything?

We know negative people. Sometimes they are our friends, and family, or maybe even us. It is to be assumed from what we have learned about mind/body connection that people who are negative are going to be more prone to illness and that people who are positive are going to spend less time being ill. Though how much of it is being positive vs. NOT being negative? Studies show that it is much more important to not be pessimistic. I personally believe that negativity, whether in words or thoughts, leads to more illness, diminished immune system and more stress. By changing our mind to a more positive state, we can change our bodies for the better. We can program our bodies to be healthy, recover quicker and even stave off illness.

I don't get sick. I just don't. When I have clients call to say they should cancel because they have a cold or a cough, I tell them to go ahead and come in. If they worry about getting me sick, I tell them not to because it isn't going to happen. I don't possess some special skill that isn't in the reality of any other person on this planet. What I have is a positive attitude and a strong will. By programming my body that I am healthy and well and not fearing every germ that goes by, I believe that I have willed myself to health. Just like I fixed the crack in my vertebrae, I can tell my body that it is not going to get sick and 95% of the time it listens.

Now, when have I gotten sick? When I am faced with repetitive emotional stress and I can't take the time between stressful experiences to mount a physical and emotional defense. I can feel it coming on and it usually has to do with uncontrollable stress when I feel helpless and out of control. What I do then is take care of my body with what it needs: extra water, vitamins, nutrients, homeopathics, acupuncture, etc. I also do visualizations activating my immune system and I give myself a deadline of when I expect to be better, and it works.

First, a word about will, which I mentioned above. My husband and I were having a conversation about why I don't get sick. There are people that take impeccable care of themselves; I'm not necessarily that person. However, if I feel anything coming on, I simply will it to go away. I'm very stubborn!

When I was in 7th grade health class we were talking about blood pressure. My teacher asked for a volunteer. It was me. (I always volunteered; I'm a sucker for that). He checked my blood pressure and then wrote on the board what it was. Now, as we know, stress is something that makes the blood pressure rise. For the next few minutes he had me stand in front of the class while he talked. That right there could raise your blood pressure. Then he announced that my blood pressure would go up if he checked it again. He explained that I was standing vulnerable in front of the class and that everyone was looking at me, staring at me and surely that stress, that attention, would cause me to stress out and my blood pressure would go up. I looked at him and calmly told him that it would be lower. The kids gasped and he just stared at me. He then told me it was impossible, there was no way it could go down. "I betcha." I said. He bet me an "A" in the class (which I was probably getting anyway). I thought about it for a second, took a deep breath and he rechecked my blood pressure. It had dropped. That was against the odds. It was true that his programming me with his words should have made my blood pressure rise. The class staring at me also should have made my pressure go up, but I willed it lower. I told you if I can't win, I don't want to play.

The influence of others is huge on our health, as we've seen in some of the previously listed studies. If someone we trust who is in a position of authority tells us something is true, we often believe it and that influences our body just the same way that voodoo death was effective.

I had a client with cancer who was doing really well on her chemo. She had energy, felt great, was exercising, having dinner guests and was basically positive and happy. She then had a scan of the tumor that showed not only was it not shrinking, it, in fact, was growing. As soon as she heard those words, her energy waned, she could no longer exercise and her optimism left. That news didn't change how she was physically feeling per se; it was just that knowledge of failure that damaged her. I wish they never had told her that the tumor was growing; perhaps she could have had healing. This is why I hate when doctors give you a timeline for death. I've seen a lot of naked butts, but I've never seen an expiration date on any of them.

There is much talk these days about Type C or cancer personalities. Even as far back as Galen he observed that women that were seen as helpless and hopeless seemed more prone to cancer. He might have been on to something. Cancer rates go up following a loss like divorce or death of a close loved one. This is from *When the Body Says No, Exploring the Stress-Disease Connection* by Gabor Mate: *Type C personalities have been described as "extremely cooperative, patient, passive, lacking assertiveness and accepting." This may resemble the Type B personality since both appear easygoing and pleasant, but...while the Type B easily expresses anger, fear, sadness and other emotions, the Type C individual, in our view, suppresses or represses "negative" emotions, particularly anger, while struggling to maintain a strong and happy façade. While we cannot say that any personality type causes cancer, certain personality features definitely increases the risk because they are more likely to generate physiological stress. Repression, the inability to say no and a lack of awareness of one's anger make it much more likely that a person will find herself in situations where the emotions are unexpressed, her needs are ignored and her gentleness is exploited.* [77] Bottom line here is to stay as positive as possible, express our feelings and acknowledge our anger.

---

[77] Mate, G. *When the Body Says No; Exploring the Stress-Disease Connection.* Pg. 125 and 127. Knopf. 2003.

Here are some summaries of studies regarding optimism and pessimism.

A 30-year study on optimism and pessimism sought to find the benefits of explanatory styles.[78] This study, which began in the period between 1962-1965, was undertaken to test the long-term effect of optimism and pessimism. The patients' answers to the Optimism/Pessimism Scale scored them as optimistic, pessimistic or mixed ES (explanatory style). In 1993/1994 when the study was restarted, the level of life satisfaction, depression, health and functioning was assessed. Overall, patients that had mixed or optimistic ES had mean scores significantly higher than average. Those labeled as pessimists reported physical scores lower than the norm and the mental health scores were lower but not statistically significant. Optimists showed 50% decrease in the risk of early death compared to those with a mixed ES. They also reported fewer limitations due to health, fewer problems with work and other activities, less pain, better health, feeling more energetic most of the time, feeling more peaceful, calm and happy most of the time. Some possible explanations are that depression and learned helplessness are less apt to appear in positive people, optimists might be more proactive in seeking and receiving medical help or it could be directly biological (changes in immune system, etc.). It is clear however, that whatever the mechanism, this study showed that there is a long-term advantage to optimism and thinking positively.

Another study sought to explore whether optimism and pessimism are simply opposite ends of the same pole or two

---

[78] Maruta, Colligan, Malinchoc, & Offord. (2002). Optimism-pessimism assessed in the 1960s and self-reported health status 30 years later. *Mayo Clinic Proceedings, 77*(8), 748-53.

separate constructs.[79] Is it more important to be optimistic or to NOT be pessimistic? This study was done with patients following coronary bypass surgery. They did several self-reported health scales, measuring pain, functional status, optimism, pessimism and quality of life. Regarding pain level, it decreased over time in patients with low pessimism over those with higher pessimism scores. The same held true for functional status and surgery-related disruption of normal life activities. Optimism alone was only related to less pain during the earliest assessed period. This particular study found that lack of pessimism, but not levels of optimism, predicted more distinct levels of recovery. They conclude that perhaps optimism may be beneficial during the early part of recovery and then the lack of pessimism is more determining of future outcomes. The most important clinical outcome from this study was that high and low pessimism was the most meaningful on surgery-related disruptions of normal activities during the year following surgery. This suggests that interventions for those who are high pessimism or perhaps, low optimism might be useful for the year following surgeries.

Kiecolt-Glaser[80] examined the effects of psychological stress on wound healing. They studied thirteen women caring for an ill family member and used thirteen controls. The subjects underwent a 3-5mm punch biopsy wound and were assessed for healing. Healing was assessed by photography of the wound and reaction to hydrogen peroxide, with healing considered final when there was no longer foaming. Beginning a week after biopsy, the wound was photographed every two-eight days until it was completely healed.

---

[79] Mahler, H, & Kulik, J. (2000). Optimism, pessimism and recovery from coronary bypass surgery: Prediction of affect, pain and functional status. *Psychology, Health & Medicine, 5*(4), 347.

[80] Kiecolt-Glaser, J., Marucha, P., Malarkey, W., Mercado, A., Glaser, R. (1995). Slowing of wound healing by psychological stress. *The Lancet,* 346, 1194-1196.

Complete wound healing took significantly longer in caregivers than in the controls, forty-eight days vs. thirty-nine days respectively. A blood draw showed that caregivers produced less interleukin-1β (regulates immune system and inflammatory responses) in response to stimulation than did the controls. Caregivers indicated significantly more stress on the perceived stress scale than the controls. The findings of this study suggest that stress-related alterations in immune function could affect the rate of wound healing. This is especially significant for surgical recovery.

Another study examined whether a pessimistic explanatory style is a risk factor for illness.[81] It was postulated that one's characteristic response to poor health might mediate the relationship of explanatory style. It was discovered that pessimistic subjects were less likely than optimistic counterparts to take active steps to combat illness. This study raises a good point of whether pessimism causes illness or whether pessimists just do not work as hard to overcome illness once they have it. Further study is warranted in this area.

A study by Ozegovic[82] sought to prove if there was a correlation between expectation of time to return to work after a whiplash injury and actual time to return. Their results found that expectation to return-to-work was not simply an indirect measure of other factors but was an influence on the recovery process. Those who had a positive return to work expectation had a 42% faster rate of recovery without further recurrence. Positive expectations lead to better outcomes. Their findings show that return to work expectation is

[81] Lin, E., Peterson, C. (1990). Pessimistic explanatory style and response to illness. *Behaviour Research and Therapy, 28*(3) 243.

[82] Ozegovic, D., Carroll, L., Cassidy, J. (2009). Does expecting mean achieving? The association between expecting to return to work and recovery in whiplash associated disorders: A population-based prospective cohort study. *European Spine Journal,* 18, 893-899.

independently associated with the self-reported rate of recovery. This suggests that modifying beliefs and expectations might improve actual recovery.

My Proposal

I propose a study to see how the programming from someone else influences the individual. We saw similar studies with the placebo effect and the doctor telling the patient what the outcome would be and then it happening. We see that interaction between client and therapist where expectation affects outcome. Siegel[83] tells stories about the power of the doctor's words in both positive and detrimental ways. What if someone's friend, family member, teacher or clergy supplants ideas? If one has a fall and the by-stander says, "Wow, you fell hard, you're going to feel that tomorrow!" does it come to pass? Or if the person would have said, "You'll be fine, you barely hit the ground." Would it make a difference? Parents make these choices in how to react to children falling down, so it should be able to work with adults as well. Perhaps it would be discovered that adult's minds are not as malleable as children.

In observing society and how easily influenced people can be in their life choices and relationships, it would stand to reason that the words people choose are indeed influencing those close to them. Designing a study charting the level of belief the participant has in the people around them and then having those people give them suggestions for health outcomes would lead to the conclusion of what sort of outside force people affect on each other. We would also have to examine individual heartiness and pessimism level to see true effects as well. Anyone want to help me do this study?

Lastly, the question was raised of why humans tend to focus on the negative as opposed to the positive. If

---

[83] Siegel, B. (1989). *Peace, Love and Healing.* New York: Harper and Row, Inc.

someone is late for dinner, the mind immediately goes to dark scenarios of that person being dead on the freeway, not simply stuck in traffic or talking at the office. What makes the mind travel straight to the catastrophic negativity? A study examining why and how the negative gains more power than the positive would be fascinating. It would also prove useful in helping people break the negative cycle and use the power of positivity for healing.

Here is a bonus study that I wanted to include, but wasn't quite sure where to put it. I'm fascinated by Dr. Emoto's work that I mentioned on page 19 so wanted to include this information here for you to enjoy as well.

Radin[84] replicated Emoto's famous water crystal study to see if intentional thoughts could affect the structure of the frozen water crystal. Over three days, 1900 people in Austria and Germany focused their attention toward water samples located inside an electromagnetically shielded room in California. Water samples located near the target water, but unknown to the people providing intentions, acted as "proximal" controls. Other samples located outside the shielded room acted as distant controls. Ice drops formed from the samples of water in the different treatment conditions were photographed by a technician. Each image was assessed for aesthetic beauty by over 2500 independent judges and the results were analyzed all blind with respect to the underlying treatment conditions. Results suggested that crystal images in the intentionally treated condition were rated as aesthetically more beautiful than proximal control crystals. This outcome replicates the results of an earlier double blind pilot test.

---

[84] Radin, D., Lund, N., Emoto, M., Kizu, R. (2008). Effects of distance intention on water crystal formation: A triple blind replication. *Journal of Scientific Exploration, 22*(4), 481-493.

So basically, saying positive things to water influenced the resulting crystal and they were beautiful. And the negative words and music made ugly crystals. If this is true, remember that our bodies are 80% water, imagine what an influence this would be on us. I recently had the honor and pleasure of meeting Dr. Emoto and hearing him speak of his work first hand. He is a truly amazing man and I encourage all of you to think of the effect you're having with your words and thoughts and check out his book *The Hidden Messages in Water*.

How to Stay Sick List,
The Keys to Unhealthy Living.

I believe that our stories become our bodies and what we say
to and about ourselves, becomes ourselves. So…if you want
to stay sick, here's how.

Tell everyone you meet
how horrible your life is.
Make it an identity instead
of an anecdote.

Find other negative people
and make them your best
friends.

Blame luck for everything,
then you have no personal
responsibility.

Say "why me?" a lot.

Live in the past, think a lot
about the bad stuff and tell
everyone.

Fear the future. You know
it's going to suck!

Take no risks to grow and
evolve.

Ask for things that will
help you and then ignore
them or do them half way.

Don't relax; after all,
you're very busy.

Make excuses like: after
the kids leave home, when
I'm older, I'm too
young…

Believe that what you
think has no effect on the
body.

Believe your
illness/sickness is
hereditary and you have
no control.

Remember there are never
EVER options for the
future.

Stay in a job you don't
like, or with a spouse you
can't stand.

Never laugh. It's for
idiots.

Resent people from your
past and blame them for
who you are now.

Put yourself down at every
turn. You truly are all
those things you say.

Tell everyone how useless
you are and use words like
"never" & "always."

Blindly take every
prescription that your
doctor gives you assuming
he has your best interest at
heart.

Surround yourself with
negativity by watching the
news and reading the
paper often.

Don't stretch, eat right,
breathe, drink enough
water, poop, exercise or
get any bodywork done.

Eat too fast when you are
stressed and upset and
don't chew.

Ask to be cured and not
healed.

Envy everyone else for
what you don't have.

Consume a lot of
chemicals in food, water,
air and home products.

Focus on all your
problems.

Try to live up to what
others think you should
be, ignoring your own
goals and desires.

Apologize for existing.

Let fear guide you and
keep you stuck.

Hold on to your anger and
negative emotions.

Try to fix everyone else;
they're broken.

***Remember, you can
never change!

How to Stay Healthy List
A Better Choice

Tell people of your successes and accomplishments. They can learn from you.

Find positive, supportive people and leave the negative behind you.

Take personal responsibility

Know that others have bad times too; you're not alone.

Live in the present moment. Don't dwell on the past or be fatalistic about the future.

Go forward into the future with a positive attitude. It's going to be phenomenal.

Take risks to grow and evolve.

When you are gifted with something you asked for be thankful and follow through.

Relax.

Don't make excuses. The time is now.

Know that what you think has profound influence on your body.

You don't have to be your heredity. Perhaps there is another choice.

There are always options for the future.

Find a way to remove yourself from bad situations like jobs or partners. Or at least, change your attitude.

Laugh.

Don't blame or resent people from your past.

Knowing that healing comes from forgiveness and moving forward.

Speak only positively about yourself.

Don't use words like "never" and "always."

Check into your prescriptions before you take them. Do your own research.

Take a "news fast" and let the paper and newscasts go for a few days.

Stretch, eat right, drink enough water, have healthy bowels and have bodywork done.

Eat slowly, in a calm environment and chew your food thoroughly.

Find true healing; don't just rely on a cure.

Take a high-quality multivitamin and mineral supplement.

Avoid GMO food.

Love deeply and feel greatly.

Eat real food and avoid processed and boxed products.

Tell the government and companies that supply our food that we want real ingredients and additives to be labeled.

Keep a food diary or try an elimination diet to see if your food might be affecting your health.

When Staying Sick is a Better Option.
Secondary Gain

I used to assume that everyone wanted to be well, that health was of primary importance. And over the years of being around several thousand people in my office and more in the world, I'm sad to say that just isn't the case. I felt like my purpose was to save everyone. "Saving the world, one knot at a time," I used to say. You know what, healing comes in its own time and for some, it might never come. Sometimes the illness is a lesson, a way of moving forward, a benefit through the suffering. I can't claim to understand the plan of the universe or God. I've seen many people become whole through illness. If they didn't have the illness, they may never have changed.

I've also seen people who hang on to every little germ as a badge of honor and an excuse to not function. We are rewarded in this society for being unwell. Look at reality TV; the least well-adjusted person is the one we're tuning into to learn about his or her failed marriage, drug addiction, hooker children, obesity and rabid dog. I really don't understand why the drug-addicted actor keeps getting attention and why we thrive on the latest celebrity breakup. Regardless of any of that, I know people, people very close to me, that don't want to change and grow and evolve.

Caroline Myss calls this "emotional currency", meaning we use our emotional issues to barter for attention and acceptance. She says we "lead with our wounds" as is evidenced in the following example. I was at a conference one year and met a woman in line for the luncheon. I mentioned that I was last in line because I was on the phone with my husband and she launched into a monologue about what a jerk her husband was and how he never paid attention to the kids and on and on. I finally suggested she might want to leave and she said she did...twenty-five years ago. She didn't really leave him energetically though. She carried him with her these twenty-five years and if it didn't already, it was going to make her sick.

I had a client that used to rejoice when her back went out because then her husband would clean the house and she could lie around and relax. It would have been so much healthier to either hire a cleaning person or simply express to him that she needed help. Now, of course, this was a totally unconscious situation. She didn't get sick on purpose, but in some unknowing way, she did.

When we were little kids there was often reward for being sick and we could use it as an excuse to not function. I spent multitudes of time in the nurse's office because I was bored or didn't want to be around children who teased me. We might have gotten comic books and special food and love from our parents when we didn't feel well; attention that we perhaps got no other time in our lives. We have to be very careful not to allow that to eek into adulthood. The consequences are much more dire than not getting perfect attendance in our permanent record.

We certainly can't say we (or others) are staying sick on purpose. Because we're not. We can perhaps shed light that secondary gain is happening. So what if you have a friend that has it within their power to get well and isn't? They won't do any exercise, they still smoke, eat crap and fight with their spouse. They still guzzle a dozen diet sodas a day and wonder why they have headaches. They haven't called the chiropractor that could fix their rib and they still haven't adjusted their workstation. Then they show up to a doctor and say fix me. I used to get so frustrated by this and almost fired a few clients over it. I would complain to my husband that I didn't want to work with people that didn't want to really get well. He made me realize, just them coming to see me for that appointment was at least one step in the right direction. We cannot take anyone else's progress personally. Remember, it's not our job to save anyone. And also a reminder to be kind to ourselves. Beating yourself up over a pattern that you are working to break or a habit that is almost on its way out is not productive. These thoughts/reactions to stress didn't appear in one moment and won't disappear that way. Gentleness, kindness and love to yourself!

Intermingled Mind and Body.
Being an Empath

This section was written specifically for fellow practitioners, but you may have these traits too. If not you, then maybe someone you know. Enjoy this section on being an empath.

Since I was a child I have felt things deeply. Perhaps many of you reading this can relate to that. I got upset in crowds feeling overwhelmed with the energy. I had trouble going to nursing homes or funerals because I could deeply feel the grief and sadness, even if I didn't know anyone in the home or those who had died.

Empathy is defined as a deep emotional understanding of another's feelings or problems, while sympathy is more general and can apply to small annoyances or setbacks.[85] But this type of empathy goes deeper. People who can actually feel others feelings or pain and help dispel it are referred to as empaths. I don't think it's possible to talk about the mind/body connection without acknowledging that other's emotions and pain can have a profound effect on us.

When I first started my practice I would take on the physical pain of my clients. I didn't know how to stop it, but I would be left feeling exhausted and sick after almost every session. I could also feel people's pain in crowds and groups of people, which was just annoying. Once I started doing Reiki, I noticed that the phenomena was greatly lessened and though I would still feel and sometimes express people's repressed emotions, I didn't take on the physical pain. Here are a few examples from my own life.

A close friend of mine at the time was in a play and as I sat in the audience waiting for it to begin I began to get anxious and nervous. My anxiety progressed to the point where I thought I was going to vomit. I knew it wasn't mine.

---

[85] Retrieved from http://www.thefreedictionary.com/empathy November 20, 2011

I got up, went back stage, found him looking sick and pale and told him to stop it, that he was making me sick as well. He confessed that he was having pretty bad stage fright all of a sudden and did some breathing exercises to calm down. As he calmed, I calmed.

My husband was doing a relay race called the Hood to Coast in Oregon. One of his co-workers was running it also and we were all shoved in a van to head to the next exchange spot. I was between the two men. About a mile from the site, I started to feel really anxious and began to get incredibly nervous. I looked over at my husband and he was calm and laid back. I was confused. Where was that coming from? I realized I was touching the legs of both runners. I turned to our friend at my right and asked him if he was nervous. He answered in the affirmative telling me he always got nervous right before a race. As soon as he got out of the van and started running, I felt fine. Now, I don't necessarily understand the point of me feeling someone else's sadness or nervousness or anxiety but wonder if it would be worse for them if I didn't dispel some of it.

Here is another example of empathy from my own practice. I was doing Reiki on a woman and she clearly had energetic issues with her throat. She couldn't wear tight necklines, turtlenecks or short necklaces. I was doing Reiki over that area and she started to get emotional. I was suddenly and unexpectantly overwhelmed with the desire to cry. Just as I started to feel that, she said, "I'm not going to cry, I'm not going to cry. I don't want to cry." So, I did. It seemed that I was channeling her feelings because they were too much for her to handle.

I think a lot of people drawn to the healing professions have abilities to do similar things. What follows in an article that I wrote for Massage Magazine about Empaths. I interviewed therapists from around the country and a lot of their suggestions for handling empathy are included. Enjoy!

Empathy or Do you Feel what I Feel?

(Written by myself and originally published at www.massagemag.com)

You're at the mall with friends and suddenly you feel overwhelmed; you have to get out of there. At a party you start to get a really bad headache and moments later the person you were talking to confesses he has a migraine. You're taking a friend to a doctor's appointment and suddenly you feel anxious and uneasy. Any of those scenarios sound familiar? These types of occurrences are common with people who are intuitive empaths.

Empaths have a deep sense of knowing. It's not that they can just put themselves in other people's shoes; they feel their blisters. They can suffer other people's pain, feel their emotions and are highly sensitive. Many people discover this skill as children and find themselves confused and overwhelmed at what they are experiencing. Some children are ostracized by their peers or told to just "suck it up" and "not to let things bother you" by unknowing parents and teachers. These children tend to be more sensitive to things like crowds and emotional movies. Bambi might not be the best choice as the child will empathize so strongly when Bambi's mother is killed that he/she might be upset for days.

Though a lot of people believe this is a skill that you are born with, some believe that it can be learned or at least honed, as you get older. Most people discover it accidently like hairdresser Marci Wolcott did. She found her skill as an adult when she was working on people's hair. "They would come in with a headache and by the time I was done with their hair, their headache was gone and I felt awful. I even took on a friend's hangover." A lot of empaths find that they are more sensitive in certain environments like crowds, near animals or with children. Hospitals, nursing homes and funeral parlors can create real problems. Many people that have this gift choose bodywork and healing as their profession.

I call this a gift, but it can sure have its negative sides. As Glen Phillips says, "Once I begin to work, I feel every pain and emotion. I accept this pain as part of my job and commitment." When this skill is first identified it can be hard to find a way to not become sick and overwhelmed. One therapist actually quit her practice during her pregnancy for fear of all the negative energy affecting her unborn child. This can be a really scary experience if you don't know how to ground the energy or keep it from overcoming you. As Laura Kamm puts it, "I've never met anyone who was authentically overjoyed by the phenomena. I am who I am and I do what I do."

When I first started doing healing work, I found that I would take on the emotions of the clients. If they were trying to hold back tears, I would find myself crying for them. I would take on anxiety of people I was sitting next to and even "went into labor" as I was holding a cat that started to birth her kittens in my lap. For people who come to us as clients, this skill can be deemed everything from weird to unbelievable to extremely impressive. Most of the practitioners that I spoke with never shared what was happening with their clients. They feel that this is just part of their job and that it's not appropriate to burden the client. If you are an empath, I encourage you to examine your motivations if you are going to start telling people about this. Some feel this skill makes them a superior healer and start to get wrapped up in the ego boost that comes from showing off. "There is a glamour to it that is unnecessary." says Suzanne Jarvis.

Benedick Howard feels that "New healers and egotistic practitioners can use this skill to manipulate clients." I caution this behavior as it borders on codependency and can lead to negative results for both you and your clients. If you are going to share, take a moment to ask yourself why.

So, you fit the description of an empath. You have the gift. Now what the heck do you do about it? Learning to feel without taking on too much is a skill that takes some practice. We certainly don't want to suffer or have to leave society because we're so overloaded. I consulted numerous practitioners and other resources to find the best way to control this energy and here are some of the answers I found:

~Meditate, specifically on the throat and root chakras.

~Be choosy. Stay away from "psychic vampires" who want to zap your energy.

~Learn to put up an "energetic shield" using your aura or chi.

~Donna Eden, in her video Energy Healing, suggests zipping up your energy like a coat and locking it by placing your tongue behind your top teeth. (www.innersource.net)

~Marci Wolcott suggests a grounding meditation or visualizing cords at the bottom of your feet attaching you to earth. She also imagines golden cuffs at her wrists that stop the energy from traveling further.

~If you feel you're taking on other's emotions, repeating your own name over and over can be helpful.

~Watch your diet as foods high in sugar and alcohol can deplete you. Protein, especially meat, tends to be more grounding than vegetarian food.

~Engage in a spiritual discipline.

~Amy Goetz imagines gold light filling her body and does slow breathing.

~Practice self-care, whether it's massage, retreats or a hot bath. The more depleted you are, the more vulnerable you are to other's energies.

~Some people rely on crystals for protection like boji stones or quartz crystals.

~Others can just "shake off the pain" by shaking their hands in the air.

~Learn to be the bad guy; it's not your cosmic responsibility to fix others.

~Find a teacher, mentor or guide. Often people appear when the time is right.

~Spend time in nature. Let the trees or the earth take the excess.

~Respect yourself. If you need a break, take it. Take the time YOU need to recharge.

~Learn energy work. After I learned Reiki I was less apt to take on a client's physical pain, but still able to instinctively find it on their body. It acted as sort of an energetic GPS for me.

~Take a break from too much negativity. Avoid the news, the newspaper and the needy neighbors for a while so you can recharge.

~Try to remain positive and realize as hard as it is sometimes, this truly is a gift that can benefit others.

As you grow and mature as a healer and acquire a stronger sense of self, you will find that the empathy grows and changes as well. You'll uncover a sharper sense of intuition and a better ability to shield yourself. I encourage you all, healer and non-healer, empath and non-empath to explore the above techniques. The only things that can come of self-exploration and evolution are positive.

Conclusion

Remember that for true health we need to balance all aspects of body, mind and spirit. And perhaps some of our physical manifestations of illness have an emotional trigger. Affirmations can help, as can meditation, doing minis and analyzing what situations we treat from a negative mindset. Our words and thoughts have a larger influence on our physicality than we realize. If we can integrate the emotions with the physical, through the techniques I discussed, we can achieve full and long lasting healing. As you can see, there are endless additions that we can make to our lives.

Healthcare and healing have always built upon what came before it. It appears to be cyclical in nature. Looking at the history and the current theories of mind/body medicine, it becomes clear that science is attempting to keep pace with people's personal beliefs about mind/body medicine. A clear example of this is the evolution of scientific thought about the placebo effect. It was first used to prove someone was faking a medical condition. It was then utilized to show if a drug was effective by way of the double-blind placebo controlled study. Now the placebo itself is used as a form of healing. This latest use is the natural progression of science, catching up with the mind/body connection that has been at work all along.

Turning to simpler, past therapies such as hypnosis, creative visualization and positive thought are contemporary ways for man to take charge of his own recovery. Ways that we can grow, heal and evolve. It is clear that scientists are interested in showing proof of what the mind can do. Triple-blind studies are being done to allow for healing from the placebo effect, and researching are experimenting with sham surgery and open vs. hidden treatments. Sports journals and business gurus are touting the effects of positive thought, affirmations and visualization. Scans of the brain are being performed to see what changes are happening inside patients when they pray, meditate, expect pain medication or are thought of fondly by their spouse. Scientists are seeing proof of what the mind can do.

With more people feeling out of control of their lives and turning once again inward, science must strive to catch up with what modern man is looking for. It seems to be more control and more power over one's health outcomes. There are currently 813,889 books available on Amazon.com that addresses the mind and body, with 1511 more to be released in the near future.[86] Our current levels of access to information are supplying material for the demands of the inquisitive. No longer are people relegated to "because my doctor said so." They are searching for other options and what they can do for themselves. Because mind/body healing is a newer topic for mainstream scientific study, it has a ways to go. But seeing research being conducted at major universities such as Harvard, University of Pittsburgh, John Hopkins University and the National Institutes of Health, shows clearly that science seeks to prove the power of the human mind. As more and more research is being done, these results will filter down to the layperson and empower them to take more personal control of their lives and choices.

At our core, we all want better health. People want cures for diseases like cancer and HIV. Or, at the very least, methods to help deal with the effects of those diseases. Every person wants more wealth, stronger relationships and a more hopeful future. The current research is showing that all those things might be possible with the right combination of thoughts and words. Learning from the negative power of the mind in situations such as hysterical pregnancy and voodoo death, it is possible to use the power of the mind for the health and wellbeing of society. If the negative can be created, then so can the positive, as is being shown by current research. There is still much to learn and not every study being done proves that the mind can control our physiology. Most of the studies, however, at least offer hope

---

[86] Retrieved July 20, 2016 from www.amazon.com.

that progress is being made. People can effect change in their bodies. If it ends up being through positive thought and affirmations, hypnosis or sham surgery, more and more people seem to be turning that way. As much as some will forever buck the system and negate whatever legitimate research is being done, at some point the mainstream has to acknowledge that the power of the mind is the power to heal. Whether we tap that power now or in 50 years, it certainly seems to be the trend for the future. We will be standing on the forefront of health!

For further study I recommend books by Louise Hay, Carolyn Myss, Dr. Herbert Benson, Dr. Norm Shealy, Dr. John Sarno, Donna Eden, Dr. David Burns, Dr. Dossey, Sam Harris, Dr. Weil, Dr. Emoto, Dr. Benedetti, Dr. John Kabat-Zin and Dr. Bernie Siegel. Also the movies *The Secret* and *What the Bleep do we Know?* And my other books, *The Alternative Medicine Cabinet* **winner of the Beverly Hills Book Awards.** (now a TV series) and Journey of Healing.

Classes are available at the Benson-Henry Institute for Mind Body Medicine at http://www.massgeneral.org/bhi/.

I would also like to thank this institute once again for providing the minis and cognitive restructuring Chart found on page 42 and 46 respectively.

Appendix A
Communication Tips

Since I am asking you to communicate with practitioners in a way you might not be familiar with I figured I'd better give you some tips and ways to avoid some pitfalls. Your honesty is important and so is your trust in the person trying to help you. So, having said that, here are a few communication tips followed by some information from someone who is a psychotherapist, Dr. Jay Fortman.

Keys to Communication

-Be as open and honest as you can with the practitioner.
-They have heard it all and don't judge what you are saying.
-They are there for you! And shouldn't be using your time to tell you their issues. An occasionally personal example as I've used throughout the book may be appropriate, but be ware of them crossing boundaries.
-Everything in your session stays confidential.
-Whoever you are seeing should be willing to tell you about their training and experience and show you proof of that training.
-Emotional releases and tears can be totally normal during this type of work, but a practitioner should never go out of their way to make you cry or force you to experience negative emotions.
-You should never be made to feel stupid or inferior. You should never be told you are wrong.
-If they are not helping you, try another practitioner. You could even ask for a referral.
-If scary negative things are being brought forth seek counseling.
-If you are showing signs of a mental break, severe depression, anxiety or are having suicidal thoughts, please talk to someone!

Sometimes communication can go wrong, or clients can get a bit too attached. Here are some words from Dr. Jay Fortman.

Whenever we interact with another individual we are not only releasing emotional but are also releasing physical energy. This cannot only affect you directly but may also create difficulties with communication between you and the other person.

Transference*, simply stated, is the reallocation of a person's thoughts and feelings about themselves or another person in their life onto you. This means that they are reacting and communicating with you as if you were the other person. This can lead to misunderstanding and/or a major communication breakdown between you and the other person. To avoid this happening, it is important to determine whether this miscommunication is a result of your transference or theirs. If the issue is yours (counter-transference) then you need to reestablish your boundaries by disengaging emotionally from the person and revisiting the problem at later time. If this is the other person's issue, then you need to recognize that it is their problem and activate your own defenses by reducing your emotional involvement in interactions with them. The next step is to quietly and gently reflect back to the person what the individual is sharing with you, using an observation such as, "you sound frustrated/hurt/unhappy about this..." If the behavior continues you may want to suggest counseling for this person.*

Codependency *is when others, including you, repeatedly attempt to rescue a person from an issue or problem they may be experiencing. Often this situation becomes complicated because you may feel a responsibility to "fix" the other person especially a friend. As a result, the communication between the other person and yourself becomes a "rescue situation" in that you may feel obligated* *to offer advice or to help this person beyond your capabilities. It is important to remember that you sometimes do not have the expertise to remedy this situation so you should suggest to the person to go to a counselor and/or support group. If this situation reoccurs it is important to reestablish your boundaries and once again gently remind the person of your suggestions and encourage them to seek help.*

Jay B. Fortman, PhD, MFT,
Therapist and Educator

Glossary of Terms

Chakras: Seven energy centers in the body, which correspond to sounds, colors and emotions. Many mind/body techniques work with the chakras. Root: red, Sacral: orange, Solar Plexis: yellow, Heart: green, Throat: blue, Third Eye: indigo, Top of Head/Crown: violet.

Chi: Life force energy, also called ch'i, qi or ki, prana, mana or vital energy. Not typically recognized in Western medicine or thought.

Creative visualization: Using pictures and imagery to program the mind and body. "A person practicing creative visualization is relaxed but the conscious mind is tuned in to listen."[87]

Guided imagery: Considered synonymous with creative visualization, but often guided by an outside source like a therapist or recorded tape.

Hypnosis: Hypnotherapy derives from the Greek word "hypnos," which translates to English as "sleep." It is the state between wakefulness and sleep. The stages of hypnosis are induction, followed by deepening and then therapy or suggestions during the hypnotic state. Seventy to ninety percent of the population can enter the medium state and less than ten percent can achieve the deep state.[88]

---

[87] Levidon, C., Leviton, P. (2004). What is guided imagery? The cutting-edge process in mind/body medical procedures. *Annals of the American Psychotherapy Association*, 7.2, 22-31. *Psychology Collection.* Web. Nov. 2010.

[88] Rajasekaran, M. Edmonds, P., Higginson, I. (2005). Systematic review of hypnotherapy for treating symptoms in terminally ill adult cancer patients. *Palliative Medicine*, 19, 418-426.

Mantram: A repeated oriental word that contained no meaning for the meditator.[89] A word repeated during a meditation, sometimes having spiritual significance, sometimes having none.

Meditation: Quieting the mind. "The highest purpose is unity and harmony, within and without."[90] "Buddhism emphasizes meditation as the only effective pathway to wisdom."[91]

Mind/body medicine: Therapeutics applied through somatic channels that strongly affect mental function and emotional state.[92] The reverse must also be true in that the mental and emotional also affect the physical.

Nocebo: A harmless substance that when taken by a patient is associated with harmful effects due to negative expectations or the psychological condition of the patient.[93]

Placebo: 1: a usually pharmacologically inert preparation prescribed more for the mental relief of the patient than for its actual effect on a disorder.
2: an inert or innocuous substance used especially in controlled experiments testing the efficacy of another substance (such as a drug).[94]

---

[89] Dossey, L. (1993). *Healing Words*. New York: HarperCollins Publishers. P 91.

[90] Knaster, M. (1996). *Discovering the Body's Wisdom*. New York. Bantam Publishing.

[91] Simpkins C. & Simpkins, A. (1997*). Living Meditation from Principle to Practice*. Boston: Tuttle Publishing.

[92] Millenson, J. (1995). *Mind Matters. Psychological Medicine in Holistic Practice*. Seattle: Eastland Press, Inc.

[93] Retrieved from http://www.merriam-webster.com/medlineplus/nocebo).

[94] http://www.merriam-webster.com/medlineplus/Placebo

Placebo effect: Improvement in the condition of a patient that occurs in response to treatment but cannot be considered due to the specific treatment used.[95]

Progressive muscle relaxation: The technique of working gradually along the body selecting one muscle group after the other, first tensing the muscles as forcefully as possible, holding the exaggerated tension for eight to ten seconds and then releasing for a longer period of time of about thirty seconds.[96]

---

[95] http://www.merriam-webster.com/medlineplus/placebo%20effect

[96] Millenson, J. (1995). *Mind Matters. Psychological Medicine in Holistic Practice*. Seattle: Eastland Press, Inc.

198

About the Author

Kathy Gruver, PhD is an award-winning author and hosted the national TV show based on her first book, *The Alternative Medicine Cabinet* (winner Beverly Hills Book Awards). She has earned her PhD in Natural Health and has authored five books including, *Body/Mind Therapies for the Bodyworker, Conquer Your Stress with Mind/Body Techniques* (Winner Indie Excellence Awards, Beverly Hills Book Awards, Global E-book Awards, Irwin Awards, Finalist for the USA Best Books Award), *Journey of Healing* (Winner USA Best Book Awards, Beverly Hills Book Awards, Pinnacle Awards and the non-fiction category of the London Book Festival) and she co-wrote *Market my Practice.*

She has studied mind/body medicine at the famed Benson-Henry Institute for Mind-Body Medicine at Harvard Medical School and has been featured as an expert in numerous publications including Glamour, Fitness, Time, More, Women, Wall Street Journal, CNN, WebMD, Prevention, Huffington Post, Yahoo. com, Ladies Home Journal, Dr. Oz's The Good Life, and First. Dr. Gruver has appeared as a guest expert on over 250 radio and TV shows including NPR, SkyNews London, Every Way Woman, Morning Blend in Las Vegas, CBS Radio, and Lifetime Television, and has done over 200 educational lectures around the world for everyone from nurses in the Middle East to 911 dispatchers in New Orleans, corporations around the US and teachers in her own backyard. She just completed work on a project for the military to create and institute a stress reduction program. For fun and stress relief Dr. Gruver does flying trapeze and hip-hop dance.

A past winner of NAWBO's Spirit of Entrepreneurship Awards, Kathy maintains a massage and hypnotherapy practice in Santa Barbara, California. She has also produced an instructional massage DVD, *Therapeutic Massage at Home; Learn to Rub*

People the RIGHT Way™ and is a practitioner with over 25 years of experience. Her award-winning book, *The Alternative Medicine Cabinet* was turned into a national talk show. More information can be found at www.thealternativemedicinecabinet.com.

Index